Marketing for Writers: A Practical Workbook

Angela Render

Foreword by Ally E. Peltier

© 2008 by Angela Render

www.angelarender.com

Published by Thunderpaw Publications

publishing.thunderpaw.com

All rights reserved.

Marketing. Internet Marketing. Sales & Marketing. Publishing. Publishing Industry. Internet Advertising. Advertising & Promotion. Handbooks, Manuals, Workbooks.

Register this book to receive free updates to the resources list and downloadable copies of the worksheets.

Visit

registration.angelarender.com

Table of Contents

Acknowledgements	1
Foreword by Ally E. Peltier	2
Introduction	4
Chapter 1 - An Overview of Marketing and Tactics	**6**
1.1 The Author's Marketing Pledge	6
1.2 Identifying Your Needs	6
Worksheet 1.2 Crafting a Mission Statement	7
1.3 Your Most Essential Marketing Tool	8
1.4 Your Most Powerful Marketing Tool	8
Worksheet 1.4 Strengths and Weaknesses	10
1.5 Platforms	11
Worksheet 1.5 My Existing Platform	16
1.6 Identifying Your Market	14
Worksheet 1.6.1 Who Is My Market	17
Worksheet 1.6.2 What Can I Offer	18
1.7 When Should You Start?	15
1.8 The Reluctant Speaker	15
Chapter 2 - Traditional Marketing Outlets	**23**
2.1 What Publishers Do	23
2.2 Book Signings	23
2.3 Print Aids	25
2.3.1 Business Cards	25
2.3.2 Brochures	26
2.3.3 Post Cards	27
2.3.4 Bookmarks	27
2.3.5 Press or Media Kit	27
2.4 Teaching and Speaking	29
2.5 Press Releases	30
Sample Press Release 1	33
Sample Press Release 2	34

Chapter 3 - POD and Me · 36

- 3.1 Viability of POD (Print On Demand) · 36
- 3.2 Who Should Consider POD · 36
- 3.3 Special Needs · 37

Chapter 4 - Marketing Shangri-La: The Internet · 40

- 4.1 A Brief History · 40
- 4.2 Web 101 · 41
  - 4.2.1 Hosting and Domains · 42
    - Worksheet 4.2.1 Domain Names · 45
- 4.3 Content · 44
  - Worksheet 4.3 Content · 48
- 4.4 Websites · 47
  - Worksheet 4.4 Nine Questions · 50
- 4.5 Blogs · 49
  - Worksheet 4.5 Blogging Topics · 54
  - 4.5.1 Blogging Platforms · 53
  - 4.5.2 Posting Tips · 57
- 4.6 Forums · 58
- 4.7 Audio and Visual Media · 59
  - 4.7.1 Podcasts · 60
  - 4.7.2 Book Trailers · 60
  - 4.7.3 Video · 61
- 4.8 Design · 61
  - 4.8.1 Programming for Accessibility · 65
- 4.9 Traffic Tracking · 65
- 4.10 Copyrights and Images · 67
  - 4.10.1 Protecting Your Copyright · 68
  - 4.10.2 Image Editing · 69
    - Sample Photo Release · 71

Chapter 5 - Getting Found · 72

- 5.1 The Secrets of SEO (Search Engine Optimization) · 72
  - 5.1.1 Relevant Content · 74
  - 5.1.2 Effective Formatting · 74
  - 5.1.3 Useful or Unique Page Titles · 76
  - 5.1.4 Links · 76
  - 5.1.5 Other Meta Tag Keywording Efforts · 77
  - 5.1.6 RSS · 79

5.1.7 Longevity	79
Worksheet 5.1 Site Focus and Keywords	80
5.2 Paid Search	81
5.3 Non-Internet Methods	84

Chapter 6 - Advanced Marketing Concepts — 85

6.1 Philosophy of Marketing	85
Worksheet 6.1 Identifying and Prioritizing Data	86
Sample Evaluation Form	88
6.2 Free Advertising	90
6.2.1 Tele-seminars	91
6.2.2 Articles and Interviews	92
Worksheet 6.2.2 Headlines	98
6.2.3 Speaking	96
Worksheet 6.2.3a Speaking Opportunities	99
Worksheet 6.2.3b Identifying Target Planks	100
Worksheet 6.2.3c Presentation Outline	101
6.3 Packages	104
Worksheet 6.3 Packages	107
6.4 Bulk Sales	108

Chapter 7 - The Marketing Matrix: Making the Aspects Work Together — 109

7.1 Coming Up with a Plan	109
Worksheet 7.1a Master Marketing Plan	115
Worksheet 7.1b Getting There	116
Worksheet 7.1c Promotional Ideas	117
Worksheet 7.1d Steps to Goal	118
Worksheet 7.1e Daily Promotional Goals	119
Worksheet 7.1f Weekly Evaluation	120
7.2 Branding	114

Resources	121
Glossary	127
About the Author	131
Index	132

Acknowledgments

    I want to extend a huge thanks to all the people who made this workbook possible: Ally E. Peltier for her friendly support and stellar editing skills, my caring supportive husband, David Lyle, who put up with many lost evenings of attention, my equally patient and loving daughter for her lost mommy time, Dr. Sheppard B. Kominars for inviting me to be his guest at Steve Harrison's Quantum Leap Program, and to the students of my marketing classes for testing all of these worksheets.

Thank you very much.

Angela Render

Foreword

Many writers are first attracted to their craft by the romantic idea of book publishing—you know, the kind of publishing where literary agents will discover you and love your book so much that they fall all over each other for the chance to spend weeks pitching it to all the top editors in town. The kind where editors bid large sums of money in order to win the right to publish you. Where a year of back and forth collaboration results in a beautiful book gracing the cover of every major magazine and the front window of every bookstore. In this kind of publishing, your book naturally flies off the shelves as the public recognizes the genius of your work and revels in your storytelling skills.

This kind of book publishing does not exist.

Sure, there was a kind of publishing heyday in which editors and authors had a symbiotic relationship of the highest mutual respect, and in which books got reviewed and authors got attention primarily due to the merit of the work. But that was a long time ago, before the biggest book publishers bought up a lot of the small ones and turned them into imprints or departments, before huge multinational corporations bought up the biggest book publishers, and before the evolution of large, national bookstore chains. These days, publishing is about the bottom line, and books are treated more like products than art by most publishers. After all, a business has to make money to *stay* in business, right?

All of this to say that, even if I've just rubbed off the false patina of your publishing dreams, your drive to be a published author should not be ignored. There is still room for all kinds of books in today's publishing environment. Better yet, new technologies such as Print On Demand (better known as POD) have made it feasible for individuals to self-publish, bypassing the maze of corporate publishing all together. Digital publishing has made it economically possible for small publishers to launch a book with print runs as small as 250 copies, thus providing for the resurgence of "Indie" book publishing. In many ways there are more, not less, opportunities to publish your book today than there were twenty years ago.

The difference is that it is much, much harder to sell them. So the modern author, the smart author, will spend as much if not more time marketing a book as he or she does writing it.

I've spent countless hours teaching my clients and students about something I call an "author's platform." Though it's a specialty of mine, I didn't invent the concept. In the publishing industry, the term "platform" refers to everything about you that helps your publisher sell your book, such as credentials, useful connections, and public presence. Next to writing ability, your platform is the most important selling point you have when approaching agents and publishers. Even a few key elements, referred to as "planks," can improve your chance of success. Without a platform, you risk your book being dead in the water. Or, rather, dead in an unopened box in the shadowy corner of a warehouse. Your publisher wants—no, *needs*—you to have a platform; it can make all the difference between a publisher writing your project off as too risky a gamble and a publisher feeling that you're a good bet. If you're self-publishing, it's even more critical to have a platform, as it will be the foundation of all your sales efforts.

While marketing a book can cost a lot of money, it doesn't have to. Again, modern technology—the Internet in particular—has made the process easier and less costly. A blog can be set up in a matter of minutes. Web domains can be reserved for as little as $5.00 per month. RSS feeds and emails can be sent to thousands of people who might want to buy your book. Don't know what all of these things are, or how to use them? Read on. This workbook will introduce the many ways that the Internet can help you to more effectively market and sell your book. It will also explain, in simple, easy-to-understand terms, what you need to do to prepare for the launch of your book. Don't the Boy Scouts always say, "Preparation is half the battle?" Maybe it's G.I. Joe.

Anyway, preparation *is* half the battle. The more work you do before you publish your book, the better your chances of success. And the more marketing you do once your book is published, the more sales you can expect. So let Angela Render be your Lieutenant—let her worksheets be your field guide. You may just come out the other end with a satisfying, lucrative career writing and selling your books. And isn't that really what you dreamed of all along?

Ally E. Peltier
Editor, Writer, Publishing Consultant
www.ambitiousenterprises.com

Introduction

If you're reading this, you're preparing to take on a beast that makes most authors shudder—marketing your own work. Maybe the only reason you're looking at this seriously is because an editor or an agent told you to. You don't really want to—after all, you poured blood and sweat into perfecting your manuscript and now you're ready to sit back and have a margarita.

Well, whoever made you read this workbook was right. The success of your book is largely dependent on your commitment to it. This is exponentially true for self-published books.

The image of the reclusive writer, eccentrically isolated in a beach house for months at a time, pouring their soul into a single earth-shattering work is ingrained in the collective psyche. A few of those authors who penned classics might have even done that. But those days are over. Most 21st century authors have day jobs. They're squeezing their writing time in somewhere between sleeping, work, quality time with a spouse, and getting the kids off to school. Chances are that many of them, you included, would rather gnaw off an arm than add marketing to their schedule, but it is an imperative.

If you mourn the lost days of quiet reflection and diligent writing, don't. Bygone authors had problems of their own. Hand writing and editing all drafts, manual typewriters, months or years between submissions of a manuscript, and a limited number of publishers. Take a moment and smile smugly at your computer, spell-checker, email program, and just think of the thousands of large and small publishers that exist today. Consider marketing the 21st century author's albatross and shoulder it. If given a choice between doing my own marketing and writing my novels out in longhand, my arthritic hand and I would choose marketing without a second thought.

Studies repeatedly confirm that the more marketing a product receives, the better it sells. The sad truth about publishing in the 21st century is that the bulk of any large publishing house's marketing budget is going to be focused on a small number of titles while the others are left to fend for themselves. Smaller publishing houses may give each title more attention, but they have less funds at their disposal.

To make sure that your title is a success, you need to take on your own marketing. The prospect can be daunting. Where do you start? What will give you the most visibility with the least amount of effort? What should you focus on? This workbook will help you tailor a marketing plan to your project by building on the skills you already have. Now, the information I impart in these pages does not relieve you of the burden of creating a stellar product. Good marketing is not a substitute for good writing. But while you create your masterpiece, if you also work toward your marketing goals, you will come out on top.

A word of warning: don't try and do everything in this workbook. The fastest way to defeat your own marketing efforts is to become unfocused, overwhelmed, and then lethargic. Select three to five ideas that fit with your own personality and background and *act on* them. Recognize your audience and learn their habits. Blogging your way to the top of the search engine results won't do you any good if your audience isn't on the Internet. Likewise, spending your time giving talks and classes is a futile effort if your target market is agoraphobic. Abandon what doesn't work and be open to new possibilities as they come your way.

I mention a number of resources in the text of this book. Links to these can be found in the Resource List at the back of the book. Since things, particularly the Web are always changing, I'm offering up to date information as well as fresh copies of all the worksheets on my website at: registration.angelarender.com.

Chapter 1

An Overview of Marketing and Tactics

1.1 The Author's Marketing Pledge

I'd like you to stand up, raise your right hand and state the following pledge in a ringing voice:

> **"I am a damn good writer. I have something valuable to offer. People deserve the *privilege* of reading what I write."**

If that sounded a little bit arrogant and presumptuous, then I think you need to repeat it until you're comfortable with the idea. Marketing in its most essential form is nothing more than cheerleading for yourself. If you don't believe the words of the Author's Marketing Pledge, then you need to look over the quality of your product because a little voice in the back of your head is telling you that something is wrong. Either that or you need therapy for low self-esteem. If you do believe the pledge, then it follows that you should take your marketing plan very seriously.

Too often, people think of marketing as trying to swindle someone into buying something that they neither want nor need. Stop thinking of it that way right now. Here's a better definition: marketing is letting people know that you exist and explaining why they should choose your product or service over someone else's. People already have wants and needs. It's your duty to let them know that you can meet those wants and needs—that you have something that might even help them. Isn't helping each other out what makes us good people?

1.2 Identifying Your Needs

Before getting any further, take a moment and set down on paper exactly what it is that you're trying to accomplish. Any business that's lasted more than a few months has a mission statement and a business plan. Writing for publication is a business and you should come up with a statement and a plan. Use worksheet 1.2 to develop your statement. Once you've defined your goals, draft a sentence in the form of a "call to action."

Worksheet 1.2

Crafting a Mission Statement

I write: *(circle one)*

    Fiction   Nonfiction   Poetry

    Novels   Articles   Short-stories   Flash Fiction

    Self-help   Memoir   Other:

My genre is: *(ex. fantasy)*

My current project is: *(ex. a children's book)*

My goal for this project is: *(ex. Newberry Award)*

What do I want from my writing? *(ex. to make a living)*

What am I willing to sacrifice to get it? *(ex. evenings and weekends)*

What am I not wiling to sacrifice to get it? *(ex. time with my family)*

Sample: To make a comfortable living through my writing for myself and my family, while still having fun with it and with my family.

This mission statement can serve as a lifeline when you get bogged down in the specifics of marketing. It helps to be able to look at it and refocus when you become scattered.

It can also be an anchor if you adhere to it blindly. Read it over periodically and don't be afraid to alter it if your goals or life situation changes.

1.3 Your Most Essential Marketing Tool

The most essential marketing tool you have is your own drive. Most marketing plans fail because the author doesn't follow through. Come up with a plan that you can live with and then *execute* it.

1.4 Your Most Powerful Marketing Tool

The reason that believing in the Author's Marketing Pledge is so important is because the most powerful marketing tool you have at your disposal is *you*. If you don't believe in your own work, then you are short-circuiting every effort you make.

You are the drive behind your own success—your ideas, your creativity, your energy, your expertise. I can't emphasize enough how important your commitment to your own success is. With you comes all of your existing skills and resources. Each of these things can be strengthened and built upon to bring in another marketing outlet.

Multichannel marketing expert, Monica C. Smith of Marketsmith, Inc. wrote in her April, 2008 newsletter that truly great brands have CEOs and executives behind them who are absolutely passionate about their products. She went on to say:

"I have learned that loving your Brand makes you want to get up in the morning and face the day. It means that you care deeply about those who touch your Brand. But a Brand is bigger than people, mistakes or a timeframe. The Brand resonates at top of a customer's mind; it's a product that they love or rely on. You know a Brand that is working when you hear someone say, "I love my iPhone," or, "I love the Mac customer service," or, "Nothing beats the GeekSquad," or, "The Frontgate catalog gives me so many ideas."

The same holds true for agents and editors. Successful books have people behind them that are in love with the book. How many of you have received rejection letters that said, "I just wasn't in love with the project?" Agents have to infect editors with passion for your work. Editors need that passion to sustain them as they sell your work multiple times to multiple people throughout the publication process. An editor can be fighting for your title for a year or more and to do that well, they must be in love with your book.

That love originates with you. You have to feel the passion in your own work and convey that enthusiasm to everyone around you. A belief in yourself and in what you write will help you take the necessary steps to build your platform and market yourself and your work.

The 16th century Chinese military strategist Sun Tzu said, "Know your enemy and know yourself." Since you are the most important resource you have, it's worthwhile to make a study of yourself and see what things you actually bring to the marketing table. Take a good look at yourself and list anything you can think of on worksheet 1.4.

Your strengths are the things that are going to get you started. By working on your weaknesses, you'll build a stronger platform from which to market your work.

Worksheet 1.4
Strengths and Weaknesses

Strength

ex. I know people

How Best To Use It

I can run ideas past my friends and infect them with passion for my project

Weakness

ex. Public speaking

How Best To Strengthen It

Join toastmasters or get coaching

1.5 Platforms

I want to include a brief note on platforms here. A platform is anything that puts your face or work in front of pairs of eyes. It can include any of the following "planks" and more:

- Print credits (such as articles, books, etc.)
- Newsletters/e-newsletters you write, edit and/or distribute
- Podcasts
- Blogs, v-logs, forums (these can be yours or those you contribute to regularly)
- Your network (both your social network and your professional network)
- Mailing lists (yours and those of partners)
- Regular speaking engagements or classes you teach
- Publicity (radio spots, interviews)
- Your educational credentials
- Book tours, talks, signings, readings

A good platform will increase your chances of attracting an agent and then a publisher. Publishing is a business. Businesses are in the habit of making money. The reason a book gets published is because a whole series of people thought that they could make money off of your work.

I mention platforms because the components of a good platform are intertwined with a good marketing plan. The platform also has another purpose: to perform the function you convinced the publisher it would do in the first place. There is a huge misconception among authors about publishers and promoting books. How many here think that once you've finished the revisions and the book is in print that it's up to the publisher to sell it? Okay, consider yourself corrected. Unless a whole host of things happen in your favor, the success of your book is still up to you. The *Guerilla's Guide to Marketing for Writers* lists 17 different conditions under which a big box publishing company might invest marketing dollars in your book. These include:

- An advance over six figures
- They thought it was good enough to be a lead title
- Your last book did well
- The timing was right

Yes, I did just include "the timing was right" in that list. All of the entries require a good amount of luck and any one of them on their own may not be enough. So unless you want to rely on the stars aligning in your favor, you need a method of hedging your bets. A platform and a corresponding marketing plan is your best path.

Small publishing houses may have the passion and commitment to promote your book, but they don't have the dollars to back it up. Anything you can do to help them, and thus help yourself, is going to make a difference.

If you've opted for a POD (*print on demand*) method of getting your work into print, you are, I hope, not encumbered by the notion that someone else will do your marketing for you. But don't think that purchasing a distribution package for your book through a POD printing house will equate to sales. It's necessary and it helps, but you still have to let people know your book exists. (See Chapter 3 on POD for more.)

Established authors are ahead of the un-established ones, because they at least have a publishing history that proves they can write. But that history can also become a ball and chain if the books didn't sell well. New guys, take note here.

Say your first book has a print run of 25,000. You sell 15,000 books, leaving 10,000 returned to the publisher. Guess how many books your publisher is going to print for your second book. The answer: probably 15,000. That's because the accounting department gets a say in how many books go in a print run. Accountants may not know jack diddly about literature, but rest assured they know how to do math.

The lack of sales on the first book may not have been because it was a poor book. Remember I mentioned timing? The sad truth is that the entire list of books that hit the shelves around the September 11th tragedy in 2001 did not sell well and there was nothing anyone could have done about it.

Pumping up your platform between books can help offset poor sales in that you can get a larger fan base together than what you had before the previous book. If your publisher doesn't believe you, then you can use that fan base to sell out the smaller print run and make them do a second printing. Your next book will be taken more seriously, not to mention you'll have sold that many more copies.

You can also use a solid platform to stage a one-week sale campaign to make your book a bestseller. This has been successfully done before. The term "bestseller" is so arbitrary as to be meaningless within the industry. It only means something to readers. There are also hundreds of best-selling markets. The *New York Times* is only one of them. You can become a regional bestseller and proudly—and legitimately—display that in your credentials. The exact number of books that you have to sell is not set in stone. It's a fluctuating number based on when the sales occurred (September is the hardest time to do it) and the number of copies other titles in your category sold during the same time period. Going back to September 11th, 2001 as an example, there were a bunch of weird titles that ended up as bestsellers because people in general were not buying books. In a small region, you could sell as few as a hundred copies in a week and be a bestseller. That isn't many when it comes down to it, especially if you have a solid platform.

Nonfiction writers are *expected* to come with a platform of some sort. In most cases, you're writing as an expert on your topic. If you've taken any classes on writing query letters, you already know that you include your credentials in the letter. These could be as little as a degree in the field. Not that I'm maligning academia. A doctorate is a good start, but if you want to sell your proposal, you're probably going to need more proof that you are capable of writing said book and that the general public will take you seriously. A radio talk show spot on your area of expertise is good, as is teaching classes in it, previous article publications…you see where I'm going with this. There are experts in every field who do not possess degrees. They are simply popularly accepted as experts. What publishers love to see is name recognition.

Traditionally, fiction writers, especially first-time authors, haven't been expected to come with a platform. It's easier for nonfiction writers because they have a built-in focus for their platform building efforts: their topic. Fiction writers have a tougher time. Thankfully, for a fiction writer, you don't have to be an acknowledged expert in your genre in order to write a novel in it. While your platform should include active participation in your genre's local groups and Internet newsgroups, you can also build your platform on planks that come from your real-world expertise, from your expertise in writing, publishing short stories, or from writer groups.

Short story authors are in an even bigger pickle. Unless you want a career publishing in literary magazines, you are going to need a solid marketing plan. The establishment gripes about shortening attention spans and how overworked Americans have less and less time to devote to reading, yet novels—especially bestsellers—continue to get longer. *Harry Potter and the Deathly Hallows* was 759 pages. Short story collections actually make more sense. Shorter fiction can be digested in one sitting. It's easier to read during mass transit hours, just before bed, or during a lunch break. Why aren't publishers snatching it up? They can't figure out how to market it.

I attended a panel discussion on short fiction at a writers conference in Washington D.C. where this topic came up. The panelists commented that the publishers needed to change their marketing. Wrong answer. You need to tell them how to market your work. You need to research your market and know how to reach your readers. You need to prove that people like you and your work. You need a platform.

Some publishers are making an effort in the direction of short fiction collections. They try and find a common thread between the stories in the collection that they can sink their teeth into and that will allow them to focus their message. Don't make them jump through that hoop. Have your marketing angle spelled out in your query letter.

Worksheet 1.5 will help you identify things you already have going for you. From there, you can choose the best direction to take to strengthen your platform. You can also begin to imagine the ways you can market to the people whose lives you touch.

Take a look at the questions on this worksheet and notice that with only two exceptions, they include interaction with other people. I'll let you in on a dirty little marketing secret: authors are in the business of selling themselves as much as their writing. Your personality and expertise are not just the driving forces behind your marketing; they are also integral features in any plan you design. After all, *people* are going to be reading your work. Not machines, and certainly not your cat.

1.6 Identifying Your Market

Now that you have a grasp of who you are and what you have to offer, it's time to figure out who might want what you have. It's best to do this exercise *before* you even write you book. There are a number of books and even workbooks available with ideas on how to sell your book. Most agree that if you want to write as a hobby, then you can write whatever book you want. But if you want to be published, you need to write the book that everyone else wants.

Before you get offended and mount your soapbox to argue how important the message you want to get across is and how much people need to hear it, take a deep breath and let it out slowly. Think. If writing that sort of book actually got results, then we wouldn't have an obesity problem in this country and cigarettes would be a thing of the past. To sell your book, you need to figure out who needs to read it, how to find them and then tailor your message so that they will want to listen to it.

Worksheets 1.6.1 and 1.6.2 will get you started. After you've outlined who, you need to contact them and learn what they think they want.

1.7 When Should You Start?

Very simple—**NOW!**

No matter what phase of the book writing or publishing process you are in, you can start on your platform. Ideally, you developed your platform along with your book. Nonfiction writers can use this opportunity to sound out their potential readers on what the readers want and then use that information to develop *their* project.

It's never too late to start. In fact, having been published a few times before will give you a broader foundation than your raw beginner colleagues, since print credits and experience with standard book signings and the like are helpful. However, starting early will allow you to build that much stronger a platform and it will allow you to recognize and take advantage of the opportunities your actions are going to bring your way.

I'd like to close this chapter with a little story about a reluctant speaker that I think illustrates the things I've covered.

1.8 The Reluctant Speaker

Four years ago, I voluntarily took myself out of the marketplace to be a stay-at-home mom. I hadn't planned to do that. I loved my job as a web developer for *Smithsonian* magazine. Talk about a prestige position! That was it, and I had a great boss, too.

Then I had my little girl. She had a giggly little smile and sparkly blue eyes. Yeah, I had a new boss. A less articulate one, granted. My ex-boss was an adult that thanked me for my efforts and said "please." My new boss tended to solve problems by stamping her foot and screaming, *"I don't want to!"*

Four years later, she was a precocious, spirited preschooler and I was faced with a decision. Do I re-enter the IT field as an out of date employee with a corresponding step back along the corporate ladder, or do I try and build upon

Worksheet 1.5
My Existing Platform

My Education: _____

Classes or Speaking Engagements I Give: _____
_____

Clubs or Organizations I Belong to: _____
_____
_____

Published Credits: _____
_____
_____

My Website, Blog, V-Log, Forum: _____

Forums, E-Newslists, or Blogs I Participate in: _____
_____

Radio, or TV Spots I Have: _____
_____

Any Other Activity that Puts Me in Front of People: _____
_____
_____

People I know Who Can Help Me: _____
_____
_____
_____

Worksheet 1.6.1
Who is My Market?

Who is my ideal customer? _____
_____

What are they like? *(Are they computer savvy? Workaholics? Poor? Strapped for time? Etc.)*
_____
_____

What do they like to do? *(go to clubs, chat on newsgroups, blog, go to the gym, watch tv)*
_____
_____

Where do they like to go? *(or do they stay at home?)* _____
_____

What do they desire most or what do they want to do?
_____
_____

What are they frustrated or angry about? _____
_____

What are they used to spending money on? *(books, food, classes)* _____
_____

How could I make their life better? _____
_____

How have I helped other people like this before?
_____
_____

Worksheet 1.6.2
What Can I Offer?

What does my customer find frustrating, angering, or desirable?	What can I offer? *(tips, coaching, book)*	What media will I use to offer it? *(ebook, CD, seminar, tips)*

the select clients I'd kept over the years—I called them my nap-time clients—and go it freelance? On the one hand, the flexibility of freelancing had its appeal, but let's face it: paid vacation, healthcare, and benefits are, well, beneficial.

After much soul-searching, I decided that, yes, I could do this. So I ran out and told all my friends, family, and clients. But…technically…I was…ah…a bit out of date. I hadn't exactly been challenged by maintaining my nap-time clients' sites and there weren't that many of them. Kids only sleep so much, you see.

Two things happened to me in a short amount of time.

First, I needed credibility, so I wrote an article with a proposal for five follow-up articles. For the first time, I had a sale—a column no less—and it happened in 14 hours.

I blinked a few times, gave myself a shake and answered the phone. You didn't hear it ringing just now? Weird. It was a business associate of my husband's telling me that the local writers' center was looking for someone to teach a class on blogging and he gave them my name. (Which, by the way, unequivocally proves the importance of announcing your doings to all of your friends and family.)

Now, the problem was that I didn't blog. I'd looked into the medium and decided that it was a profound waste of time. Those posts would make excellent, sellable articles. Why give them away? I'd also never taught a class before. But what can I say? I'm a trained researcher, web geek, and a really fast learner and blogging software is easy to use. I could learn to do it by the fall, no problem.

I said, "Sure, I can do that." When they asked about me and my background, I sort of skirted the lack of actual blogging experience and emphasized the articles I'd sold and all my other experience. They got excited and I thought, good deal.

They said, "Send us the write-up for our catalog. It goes to press in ten days."

"For the blogging?" I asked.

"All of it," they said.

Uh oh.

So I scraped my jaw off the floor, ran home and called a friend of mine who has 50 years of experience teaching classes and giving talks.

I said, "Can you help me?"

You see, I get up in front of people to give a talk on a topic and my brain takes all the stuff that I know and hides it from me. If my facts would stay where I put them, I'd be a lot more comfortable.

He said, "Angela…hey! Come down off the ceiling. You just need to join Toastmasters."

"Is that a club?" I asked.

"Yes. It'll give you practice and they'll give you pointers."

After much convincing, I said okay and got to work preparing the course materials…and taking care of my clients…and my daughter.

Did I join Toastmasters?

No, I did not.

I did what every self-respecting Render would do given the same situation. I pulled myself up by the bootstraps in the finest Rooseveltian tradition and plowed into it cold.

The day of my teaching debut arrived with all the pathos of a dramatic comedy of errors. Three cups of high-octane coffee. Bumper to bumper traffic. Arriving late. No parking. No lunch.

I unloaded my laptop with its beautifully prepared PowerPoint presentation and strode toward the building like a prisoner on the way to her own execution—a prisoner who hadn't even had a lousy last meal. I found my can-do attitude slipping. Instead of that positive little voice in my mind saying, "I think I can, I think I can," I kept hearing a four year old screaming, "*I don't want to!*"

I walked up to the receptionist and said much too brightly, "I'm here for Blogging For Beginners."

She said, "Room 105. Downstairs."

I lugged my laptop down the stairs, found the room. It was picturesque and just what one would expect in a writers' center. One wall was completely covered with full bookshelves. Tables had been set up in Camelot fashion. The 17" monitor I'd requested was waiting on the table. Relaxing a little, I started to set up. I looked around. Where was the power outlet? They knew I was giving a PowerPoint presentation and even supplied that nice monitor. I dug through the bookcase, looking along the wall. Was this place built in the 1800s? I felt the start of a good solid ulcer in my stomach.

My students began arriving. I excused myself, apprehension growing, and dashed back to the receptionist.

"There's no power down there!" I wailed.

She gave me a disbelieving glare and went to look for herself. Thusly slapped in the face with the truth, she promptly moved us into the auditorium while I got several bottles of liquid energy from the vending machine. With hands that shook, I got my computer and the monitor set up. On a table. Fifteen feet away from my poor students because that's as far as the extension cord would reach across the stage.

I finished off my first 20oz of caffeine.

I whipped out my thirty pages of beautifully scripted security blanket and held it aloft like a knight going into battle. With my free hand I gripped the table that held my laptop so hard I buckled the laminated particleboard. I smiled brightly and introduced myself. My legs wobbled. My heart pounded. I cracked open the second 20oz and took a swig. This was going to be a long three hours. I launched into my script.

I honestly couldn't tell you much about that presentation other than that I smiled. They laughed at the right scripted places, asked questions that I apparently answered to their satisfaction, and I downed three 20oz bottles of soda. I even got good feedback, though every last one of them said that I spoke too fast. But I made it through and got invited to come back to teach the next semester. Yes. I just *had* to drug myself to get up in front of fifteen people and act like an expert.

Well, I *am* an expert. I just have trouble talking about it outside of a party situation.

But I did it and I survived the experience. If you believe in your work, you will be able to take the steps necessary to persevere. Believe me. I've been there. Thankfully, you don't have to use my methods to accomplish your goals. You don't need toxic doses of caffeine, or risk having to join AA either. You can actually take advantage of the organizations around to help you *before* you have a deadline. And if you're a painful introvert or a reluctant speaker, Toastmasters really will help.

Chapter 2

Traditional Marketing Outlets

2.1 What Publishers Do

Publishers have been marketing books for more than a century, but they're limited on both time and money. Because of this, they tend to stick to tried and true methods of promotion. These will most likely include:

- A listing on the publisher's website
- The publisher's catalog
- Advanced Reading Copies (ARC's) to booksellers, subsidiary rights buyers, and key media people
- Review in *Publisher's Weekly* and *Kirkus Reviews*
- Publicity kit sent to the *New York Times*, *USA Today,* and a few, select newspaper book-review sections in target markets
- Book tours
- Radio or other media interviews
- A postcard mailing to a large list if you provide it

> **Quick Vocabulary**
>
> Prospect: Someone who may be interested in purchasing your book.
>
> Customer: A person who has purchased your book.
>
> Conversion: Turning a prospect into a customer.

That isn't very much when it comes right down to it. In fact, with two exceptions, there isn't anything listed that you couldn't do yourself. The only thing publishers have over you is experience, connections, and name recognition.

2.2 Book Signings

Book signings and appearances are obligatory whether you self-publish or not. It has been my experience that sales are directly related to the number of people who come through the door. Therefore, advertising your appearances is imperative.

The Authors & Speakers Network has a great list of 40 tips for making your signings count. Many of the tips address what I would call professionalism. They deal with appearance, behavior, courtesy, and taking responsibility for making your event a success. For example:

- Don't sit behind the table and glower at people
- Send out press releases to advertise your event
- Bring your own signs
- Be nice to the host
- Ask the host for a list of media contacts to add to your own
- Hand out full color bookmarks or postcards at the event so people can buy later
- Have a presentation to make

I think the press releases and presentation ideas are the most valuable tips of the 40. You can't count on the store to advertise your event. I had one signing where the owner completely forgot about it, didn't advertise it to customers, and wasn't even present in the store when I arrived. This was in spite of my calling and emailing the owner to discuss details. Letting your list know about it as well as the conventional media outlets is important. If the event is near a university, put up fliers—on campus and in the local coffee shops. Call any pertinent department and let the deans know. They might offer class incentive to attend, especially if you're an alumnus.

As for the importance of the presentation, ask yourself this: do you have sufficient name recognition in the region of your signing to draw a crowd on your name alone? I certainly don't. Sending out a press release like, "Local author and historian Angela Render holds singing for her historical novel, *Forged By Lightning: A Novel of Hannibal and Scipio*…" drew a crowd of one. He was a history buff and the title caught his attention. That press release offered a talk on military history and a chance to see some reproduction weaponry, too. Live weapons. You'd think that would be a decent draw for a war novel. But it wasn't enough.

What did draw a more respectable crowd was the promise of food—desserts from ancient Rome and Carthage, to be specific. That one included a presentation targeted to the specialty bookstore it was given in, too.

The best turn-out I had was for a group reading held through the Maryland Writers' Association Baltimore Chapter at a local library. This event was well advertised, was sponsored by several groups, and featured five local authors. Consider banding together with authors of similar topics and doing joint appearances to improve your reach.

An author I spoke with at a science fiction convention had another clever idea. He discovered that there was a regular group that met at the bookstore and pitched a presentation to them. This virtually guaranteed him an audience. An added bonus was that the group's presence and interest in his presentation attracted the attention of random customers in the store far more easily than a guy sitting at a table would.

2.3 Print Aids

There are a few printed materials you should have at hand to promote yourself. Many of these things you can design and print yourself, but keep in mind that they are a professional representation of you and your work. The money you save by designing your own instead of hiring a professional could cost you two or more times as much in time and in lost sales.

2.3.1 Business Cards

Business cards are beyond doubt the handiest and least expensive marketing tools you can have. They're portable, have all your pertinent contact information on them, are essential in any networking event, and can even be handed out as bookmarks or emblazoned with event advertising stickers on the back and left at bookstore cash registers for clerks to stuff in bags.

Your business card should include the following information:

- Your name
- Website url
- Email address

Book business cards should also include:

- Book title
- ISBN
- Publisher
- A picture of the cover (if possible).

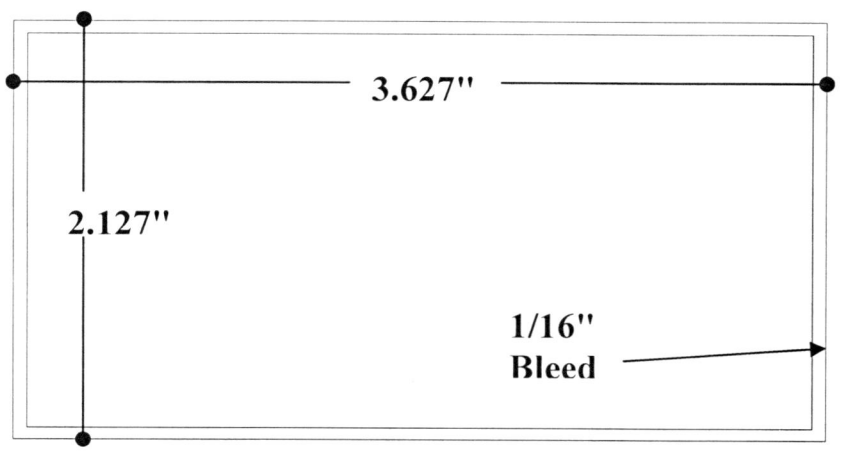

Avoid creating a business card that is all graphics with only a website url on it. Most people won't bother to go there and find out what the card is for. The same holds true for the secretive minimalist approach.

This is a means of conveying information. Put the information on the card.

Attractive, full-color, glossy business cards can be purchased for as little as $10/100. I use Overnight Prints and I've been very happy with the quality and the service. Some online printers will have templates you can use for your cards, but I recommend that you hire a professional to design a pretty one for you. If you're good with Photoshop, you can try your hand at it as well. The type of file most printers are looking for is a 300dpi .tif, .jpg, .eps, or PDF.

2.3.2 Brochures

Brochures are handy tools to have when giving lectures or if you have a table at an event. They're particularly important if you are promoting your book as part of a bigger package. (We'll discuss packages in Chapter 6.) A brochure can be as simple as a single page with your book cover, back cover or marketing copy, and upcoming appearances. A more useful brochure is a full color tri-fold affair with a catchy, provocative title and useful information tidbits inside. It could include:

- Speaking topics and opportunities to hire you
- Short reviews or testimonials
- 5 catchy tips that address a desire of your target market
- Your picture
- Your book cover image

To be effective, it must also include your website url and email address.

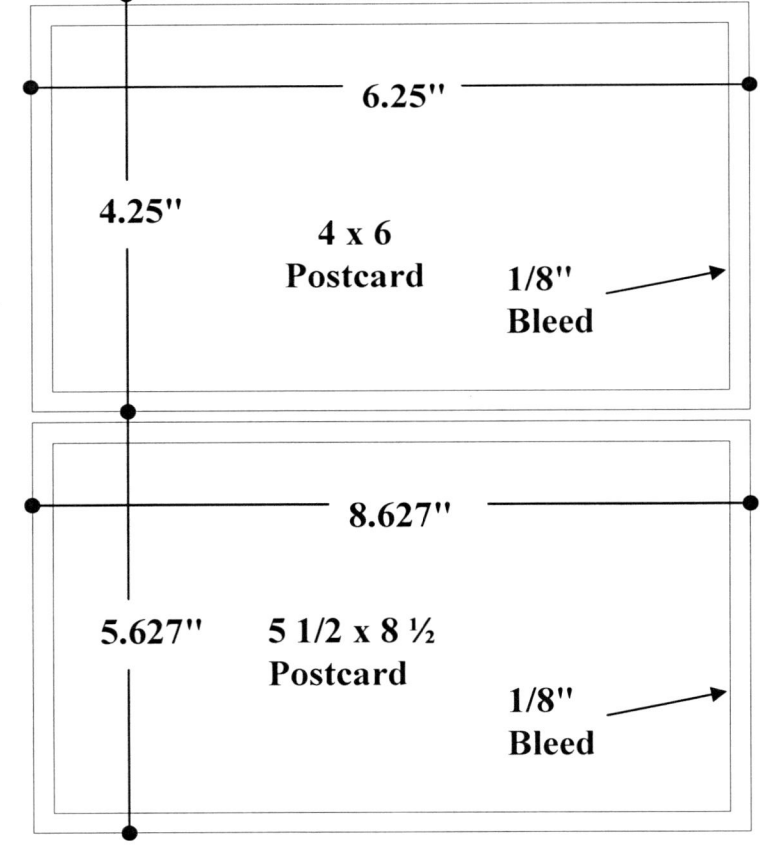

Unless you're attending a convention where you'll hand out these things by the thousands, it's most cost effective to invest in a full color laser printer. At $1 a side to have color copies made for you, you'll pay for the cost of a printer at 250 brochures. To get your printing costs below $1 a page, you have to purchase quantities of 500 or more. In most cases, you'll need to change your information before you've handed out all 500.

2.3.3 Post Cards

Post cards are useful at shows and signings because they can be treated like more informative business cards. Post cards can also be mailed out to announce your appearances and make special offers. They come in two standard sizes: 4 x 6 and 5 ½ x 8 ½. Full color one-sided 4 x 6 cards can run $30/100, making them far more expensive than business cards. The type of file most printers are looking for is a 300dpi, .tif, .jpg, .eps, .PDF.

2.3.4 Bookmarks

Bookmarks are nice giveaways at signings, fairs or any other place you're promoting your book. They should contain the same information as a book business card:

- Your name
- Website url
- Email address
- Book title
- ISBN

Unlike a business card, they should be more graphically interesting. Make it something someone would want to use and would like to look at. One pitfall I've seen on the bookmarks I've collected at conventions is that they are so graphically interesting that I can't tell what the book is. I can't find the title or the author's name. While attractive, these bookmarks are not performing their primary function which is to promote you. In this instance, I recommend you hire a professional.

2.3.5 Press or Media Kit

A press kit, or media kit, is another essential piece for your marketing stockpile. Despite what the name implies, the press are not the only people interested in seeing your press kit. Bookstore promoters want that information as do event coordinators. The purpose of your press kit is to tell people who you are, what you do, and why it will matter to an audience or readership. It should also include any incidentals that a person doing a story on you would want access to, such as a biography, quote, picture, etc.

Press kits have traditionally been handed out or mailed in print format, but in this age, it's useful to have an electronic copy available for emailing and download as well.

A press kit might include:

- Your author bio
- The back cover copy from your book
- Published reviews
- A schedule of your upcoming appearances
- A list of interview questions to ask you
- Press releases
- Relevant publicity clips about you or your book
- Clippings that prove your topic is newsworthy
- Book fact sheet including the book's title, publisher, ISBN, page count, publication date, and price
- Glossy full color book cover
- 5 X 7 professional author portrait photo
- Business card, bookmark, flyer, post card, brochure, or other marketing materials
- Sometimes a review copy of your book
- Audio or video clips of you (CD/DVD for print copy, downloadable file for web)

Something this complete would not be mailed in its entirety cold to a media contact. It's too overwhelming and would be thrown out unread. All of these items should be available on your website under a press kit heading. The files can either be compiled into a single PDF (*portable document file*), or broken up into several with print quality photo files of your book cover and of you available for download as well. Print quality is 300 or 600dpi.

When sending printed copies out, target very carefully who is to receive them. Research the person and the venue and then craft a cover letter that addresses that person's needs specifically. Printed media kits should be bound in a glossy good quality two-pocket portfolio folder. Attach a copy of your book cover to the front. If you have the budget, you can have special folders printed for you.

Many media contacts work solely via email. The most successful e-media kits are worked into the body of the email as HTML pretties. If you're not a programmer, find someone who can create one of these for you, or look for a bulk email sending house that has ready-made templates for you to use. Do not email a PDF, (*portable document file*) .doc, .zip, or any other attachment to a contact cold. SPAM and virus filters strip off attachments, especially large ones. Put the cover letter first and then offer to send a PDF to them, or invite them through a clickable HTML link to visit your website and download a copy.

The object of a press kit is to have everything someone would want to know about you available in one easy place. You should update your press kit frequently.

As for who should receive your media kit, you are going to mail the expensive copies to agents, editors, and media contacts whom you have researched thoroughly and who you know are interested in your topic.

2.4 Teaching and Speaking

The most lucrative method of promoting yourself is through your personal appearances. Where you give these talks will depend greatly on your topic. Toastmasters is a great resource both for learning the fine art of presentation and for discovering hidden opportunities. I've had great luck getting started with the following resources:

- My local writers' center
- My local writer's associations
- Through my clients
- The local chambers of commerce
- Business women's associations
- Local parks and recreation
- Continuing education programs through the community college

Keep an open mind and look around at your local clubs and organizations. Most have monthly meetings that will feature a guest speaker. Think about how your topic can be tailored to suit their needs and interests.

For this venture, you'll want a speaker's kit. A speaker's kit will have much of the same information as a press kit, only it will be tailored to reflect your speaking experience. It will also include:

- A list of speaking titles/topics
- An audio or video clip of you

- A "one-sheet" – a two-sided page of information (most likely this will have a two page version that can be easily faxed to event coordinators). It will include:
    o A picture of you
    o Quotes from people who have heard you speak
    o A bulleted bio
    o A client list or places your book is sold
    o Titles and short paragraphs about the topics you speak on

The person in charge of setting up speakers is usually the events coordinator or program director, though for smaller organizations it may be the secretary or even the president. For more on Speaking, see section 6.2.3.

2.5 Press Releases

The most often abused marketing tool is the press release. I say it's abused because most people treat is as a simple announcement of what they're doing. It should do that, but it should be worded in such a way as to make someone care. I'm including a sample press release for you to look at, but when composing your own, never lose sight of the fact that it's supposed to inspire a person to act on your behalf. This action could be to purchase your product or service, hire you to speak or, most likely, write an article on you and your book.

The most effective press release will be tailored to a target media outlet. You need to research what they do and who their audience is. Then come up with a reason why they should spend time on you and your book. Program directors and publication editors, while wonderful caring people, don't care about you or your book. They care about selling advertising. To sell advertising, they need to have a growing and happy audience.

> **Quick Vocabulary**
>
> Sound Bite: A short piece of speech taken from an interview or speech as the "essence" of what that speech was about.

Your job is to tailor the press release in such a way as to convince the media that your information will be of interest to their audience. You're looking for an angle on your topic. Your information needs to address one of a human's basic wants. It must offer to make them one or more of the following:

- Happier
- Healthier
- Wealthier
- Sexier

Editors and program managers are chronically swamped and short on time. Your press release needs to make their jobs easier. Make it clear, concise, and relevant. Make your contact information easy to see. Do as much of the legwork for them ahead of time as you can. This could include possible program or article titles, captions or a written version of a sound bite.

Two important points to make are:

- How interviewing you will make their audience happy
- Why they should interview you now

I had the privilege of working for *Smithsonian* magazine from 2000-2004. During my time there, Don Moser, the editor for 21 years, retired and Cary Winfrey, formerly of *People* magazine, took the helm. Don had always looked for interesting angles on whatever topic they were covering. Cary was no different, but he added a mandate that Don had never insisted upon. Cary asked the question, "Why should we print this story now?" Don loved timely stories, but he made room for the "evergreens"—stories that were timeless. Cary insisted upon "timely" and only if they needed an extra story would an "evergreen" get in there. While we tend to think of *Smithsonian* as a timeless magazine held to a higher standard, Cary does have a point. If it's evergreen, it'll keep 'til later. Give me something newsy. This is doubly true for popular magazines, triply true for weeklies and ten times truer for dailies and for television.

I cover free publicity (and press releases) in more depth in Chapter 6, and Worksheet 6.2 will help you set down some catchy ideas and time pegs to use in your press releases. But here are a few guidelines to get you started:

- Include all of your contact information (address, fax, phone, email, website)
- Have an exciting headline
- Your lead paragraph should cover who, what, when, where, why, and how
- Put the most exciting or relevant information about you or your book first, then list any other ideas or information in descending order of importance
- Use bulleted lists for your key points
- Put your book's technical details last (title, author, publisher, price, ISBN, number of pages)
- Don't send a headshot or book cover if you have a more exciting (relevant) action shot, and include a ready-made caption

- Let them know a media kit is available on your website
- Include a short bio at the end

With the changing needs of the media and the subjective nature of what they cover, an idea that was rejected once might be accepted several months later. An event that makes your story important could happen, or the person you submitted it to could have left for another job and their replacement might love your idea. Keep your press releases up to date and keep submitting them.

I've created two sample press releases about *Free to be Flexible: A Guide to a Long, Happy Life*, a hypothetical book on yoga. If there really is a book by that title, I claim ignorance of its existence.

Sample 1 is what most people think of when they think of a press release. Sample 2 is what will get you noticed.

Notice the differences between the two. The first one is focused on his book, while the second draws attention to the key human interest points: live longer, be happier, be more focused, have more energy. Dr. Doe even provides short quotes that could be used as sound bites. What's more, the second is focused on an event that the media will probably want to cover anyway.

The second press release hands the media people an angle on the story that is fun and unique. He's also offered to do interviews. This press release could be published as-is, and, altered a little, it could target morning talk shows in addition to local newspapers and magazines. Morning radio programs might give him a short segment as well.

I got a bit excited about this book myself while writing the second press release. And emotion is what good marketing is all about—your enthusiasm about your work and your ability to infuse others with that same passion. What good press releases and cover letters are about is making the jobs of the people you're contacting as easy as possible. Have everything they could ever need available to them and easily acquired.

Inclusion of logos is intended to spark ideas, not imply the endorsement of the organizations represented.

Sample Press Release 1

FOR IMMEDIATE RELEASE
April 1, 2008

Contact: Dr. John Doe
Day Phone: 555-555-5555
Cell Phone: 555-555-5555
jdoe@yogaforlife.com
www.yogaforlife.com

Dr. John Doe Holds Demonstration and Book Signing

New York – April 1, 2008 – Local author and fitness guru Dr. John Doe promotes his new book, *Free to be Flexible: A Guide to a Long, Happy Life* at this year's New York Festival. The book covers how yoga has evolved through the ages. Its illustrated pages provide tips and information as well as ten sample workouts.

Dr. Doe received his medical degree from George Mason University in 1975. He has practiced yoga for sixty years. His articles on the health benefits of yoga have appeared in *JAMA* and the *New England Journal of Medicine*. His previous book, *Yoga and Me*, is available on amazon.com.

"People underestimate the value a few simple poses a day can have for them," Doe claims. "People claim to want longer lives, yet they cringe at the thought of spending years on bed-ridden life support. Yoga provides a fun, easy way to stay active every day of your life. It also improves circulation, relaxes the body, relieves stress, and contributes to an overall feeling of wellness."

Attendees at this year's New York Fair will have the opportunity to "pose" with the doctor and not just for photographs. Dr. Doe will hold a demonstration of his favorite fast workout. "The poses will be fun and suitable for all ages," he claims. "Participants will leave feeling better than when they arrived."

Between demonstrations, Dr. Doe will be available to answer questions and autograph copies of his new book.

Free to be Flexible: A Guide to a Long, Happy Life (ISBN 1-555555-55-5) Publisher, PO Box 555, New York, NY, 11360. 250 pages. Copyright 2008.

Sample Press Release 2

FOR IMMEDIATE RELEASE
April 1, 2008

Contact: Dr. John Doe
Day Phone: 555-555-5555
Evening Phone: 555-555-5555
jdoe@yogaforlife.com
www.yogaforlife.com

Discover 5 Easy Moves For a Longer, Happier Life During the New York Fair

New York – April 1, 2008 – Think there's no time for fitness? There's plenty of time if you practice yoga. Come watch 86-year-old Dr. John Doe twist his way through a fun, exciting demonstration at this year's New York Fair. Studies show that twenty minutes of yoga a day makes people:

- Live longer
- Have a more positive outlook
- Focus better
- Feel more energetic
- Feel less stressed

"People underestimate the value a few simple poses a day can have for them," Doe claims. "Yoga provides a fun, easy way to stay active every day of your life."

Attendees at this year's New York Fair, to be held April 30, 2008 at the New York Fairgrounds, will have the opportunity to "pose" with the doctor and not just for photographs. Dr. Doe will hold a demonstration of his favorite fast workout. "The poses will be fun and suitable for all ages," he claims. "Participants will leave feeling better than when they arrived."

Between demonstrations, Dr. Doe will be available to answer questions and autograph copies of his new book, *Free to be Flexible: A Guide to a Long, Happy Life*. The book covers how yoga has evolved through the ages. Its illustrated pages provide tips and information as well as 10 sample workouts.

Sample Press Release 2 (cont.)

Dr. Doe received his medical degree from George Mason University in 1975. He has practiced yoga for sixty years. His articles on the health benefits of Yoga have appeared
in *JAMA* and the *New England Journal of Medicine*. His previous book, *Yoga and Me*, is available on amazon.com.

Dr. Doe is available for in-person and telephone interviews. Contact him at jdoe@yogaforlife.com or by calling 555-555-5555. More information on him and his book, including a press kit, are available on his website at www.yogaforlife.com.

Free to be Flexible: A Guide to a Long, Happy Life (ISBN 1-555555-55-5) Publisher, PO Box 555, New York, NY, 11360. 250 pages. Copyright 2008.

Chapter 3

POD and Me

3.1 Viability of POD

POD (*print on demand*) has been around for a number of years, but has carried a stigma. Self-publishers were the first to take advantage of this technology and self-published books have been looked down upon as books that weren't good enough for a traditional publishing house to publish. That stigma is disappearing and traditional publishing houses are even offering copies of out of print books through POD.

POD simply means that a copy of a book is not printed until it is purchased. Traditional publishing houses attempt to guess how many copies they can sell, then they do a print run. If they guess wrong, they are forced to accept the return of the unsold books. POD eliminates a lot of waste both in time and in paper.

One of the biggest benefits of POD is the return on book sales. With many printers, you pay only the cost of printing the book plus shipping. You set the list price and pocket the rest. That's a far better deal than you would get from a traditional publisher.

The problem with POD is distribution. If you purchase an ISBN, most POD printers will list you on Ingram. Ingram is a wholesale distributor and if you're listed with them, you can have your books sold through Amazon.com and through brick and mortar stores…in principal. In practice, you can get your book listed on Amazon.com without Ingram and a listing in Ingram does not mean that you will see your title at your local big-box chain store. It simply means that they can order a copy upon request. Someone still has to convince the stores to put your books on their shelves.

3.2 Who Should Consider POD

You should consider POD if you:

- Have a clearly defined market
- Can easily reach your market
- Are a recognized expert on your topic

If this sounds like identifying and establishing a platform and marketing plan then give yourself a gold star and move to the head of the class. I opted for

POD with this workbook because my students kept asking for it and I needed it quickly. This will not, however prevent me from shopping it around to agents and publishers.

POD for fiction writers basically requires the same things:

- Know how your market can be reached
- Establish ways of using those outlets
- Know why you were the perfect person to write your novel

Fiction writers, keep a sharp eye on your national genre organizations and pertinent conventions. You can become a panelist at some of these simply by volunteering and mentioning why you should be there, and the why doesn't necessarily have to do with what you wrote about.

There is another reason to consider POD and that is to test-market your book. Since POD is fast and inexpensive, you can print out a few copies and even have multiple looks or titles. These copies can be sent to contacts on your platform. You can walk around the local Starbucks and ask people what they think of your title or the cover, or the concept, or the back cover copy. This "sneaker research" can be reported on your book proposal.

Will publishing your book POD destroy your chances of attracting a traditional publisher to your project? Absolutely not. Traditional publishers figure that they can reach a broader audience than you've already marketed to, and your sales success and market research can mitigate the gamble they would take on your book.

3.3 Special Needs

If you do opt for POD it is absolutely essential that you have a solid platform, a good marketing plan, and the drive to make it happen. My first book, a historical novel called *Forged by Lightning: A Novel of Hannibal and Scipio* was a POD. It's only sold a little over a hundred copies, and I'm here to tell you that its lack of sales is completely my fault. You are about to be the beneficiaries of my classes at the school of hard knocks.

My first failure was a lack of research into my market and a complete absence of a platform. I did, however, have a marketing plan. Not a stellar one, but a solid one. Did I execute my marketing plan? Nope. I got as far as the website and a couple of book signings. I am building my platform now with my eye toward my next book. I will do some market research with my current book and then shop it around for a publisher at a later date. Because marketing a

POD book is the responsibility of the author and authors have traditionally been lousy at it, a poor POD sales showing isn't as devastating to an author as a poor sales showing for a book published through a traditional publishing house. A stellar sales rating through POD will benefit you if you choose to shop it to a publisher, but if you're selling well on your own, why would you? $10 profit per copy sold is a lot better than the $.90 royalty you'd get on a $15.00 retail book.

There are a few things you need to do for yourself if you decide to go POD. One of the best things you can do is to become an independent publisher. In order to be considered a publisher, you must own your ISBN. You cannot purchase one through your POD, though Lulu and some others will sell you one. To get an ISBN, you can purchase a single number for $125, or a block of 10 for around $275 dollars through R.R. Bowker (www.isbn.org). You must also purchase Bowker's SAN (*Standard Address Number*) for $150.

Bowker has other services such as bar code generators, access to adding or editing your title in *Books in Print* (a catalog shopped by retailers and libraries) and other useful tools and information. The rest is accepting the responsibility for the complete publication, marketing, sales, and distribution process. Simple, right?

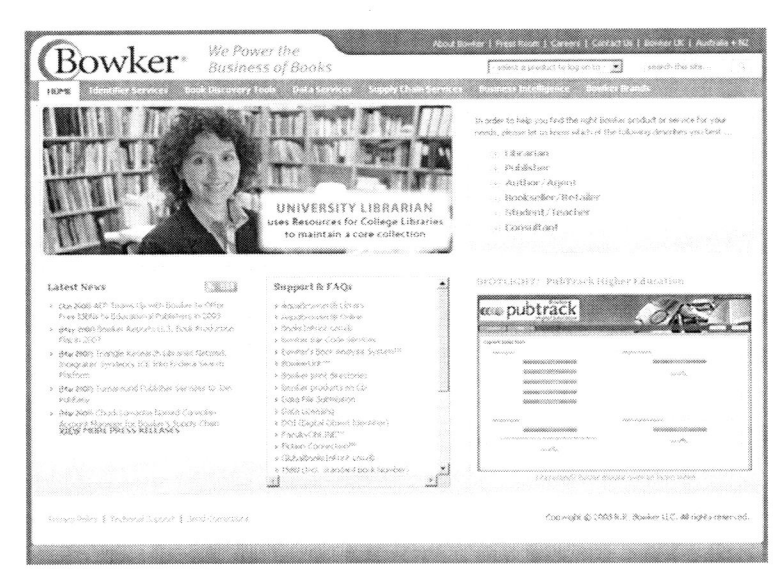

Luckily, there are services that you can purchase for every aspect of the process, including hiring a PR person, and I recommend that you hire a professional for at least some of the process. Cover design, layout, editing, and even distribution are things that you may not want to take on. Most POD printers offer these services a la carte.

As for the marketing, even if you hire a PR person, you are still going to be responsible for the bulk of it. You need printed reviews from reputable sources. Some of these reviewers won't even look at your book unless it's sent from a publisher (*Books in Print* is one of those). If you've built your platform correctly, you will already know which publications you need to be reviewed in and if you've turned yourself into an independent publisher, you can submit to them yourself.

Awards can propel a book into super-star status. In order to even be considered for some of them, the organization needs to receive a pre-publication copy of the book. For a traditional publisher, this would be a galley. For you, it means delaying the release date of your book by 1-3 months. Research the awards you would like to apply for and read their guidelines. Plan ahead.

The biggest hurdle is getting your book in brick and mortar bookstores. That means loads of sales calls and possibly a financial investment to attend book shows. BookExpo America is one of the biggest and will draw retailers, buyers, librarians, and even TV and movie producers. Finding an organization that has a table at one of these things and hitching a ride is worth looking into. The Independent Book Publishers Association is one of these groups.

Chances are, though, that you can write off seeing your title in all but your local bookstores. Count on your sales to come from amazon.com, book chain websites and from personal sales through you. Offering affiliate incentives to sell your book for you is a great way to make money. You may have to offer up to 50% of your profit, but I think that's an acceptable deal for not having to do any of the sales work.

Inclusion of logos is intended to spark ideas, not imply the endorsement of the organizations represented.

Chapter 4

Marketing Shangri-La: The Internet

4.1 A Brief History

First, I'm going to give my two minute overview of what the web is. The World Wide Web is an international collection of electronic images and documents with absolutely no organization or order to them. It's called the web because these documents reside on a vast network of computers linked together by a bunch of stringy phone lines. Yeah, I know there's DSL, fiber optic, T1s, cable modems, satellite, wireless, and all these buzz words for fast connections. So some of them are faster than others. It's still the phone. The web is distributed by an international collection of computers networked together and using a common protocol: the Internet.

Because web resources are jumbled together all higgledy-piggeldy, services sprang up to try to create order.

The Internet is descended from ARPANET, a concept first published in 1967. The purpose was to communicate with and share computer resources among mainly scientific users at the connected institutions—primarily universities, but also research facilities. Developed under the direction of the U.S. Advanced Research Projects Agency (ARPA), the web was realized on a small scale in 1969.

ARPANET was handed over to Defense Data Network, and a network of scientific and academic computers funded by the National Science Foundation in 1970. It then became known as DARPANET.

Popularized in 1993 when the first browsers became available and made the information more accessible, the Internet was released from government control in 1995. Today, the Internet is still a network of individual sources of

> **Quick Vocabulary**
>
> Internet: An international collection of computers that are networked together using a common protocol.
>
> Web: One aspect of the Internet. Short for *World Wide Web*, it is a collection of computers displaying information via and HTML protocol.
>
> Email: Messages sent through the Internet.
>
> FTP: *File transfer protocol*. A method of sending file packets through the Internet.
>
> IM: *Instant messaging*. a text-based computer conference over the Internet.
>
> IRC: *Internet relay chat*. An Internet service that enables participants to chat in real time.

information and is a valuable research and communication tool. People also use it for entertainment, shopping, and community.

The reason I told you all this is to establish that despite the commercial uses of the Internet and its interest to business, the people using the Internet have certain expectations. One huge expectation is that there will be lots and lots of free information available to them. Now the reason I told you that was because fulfilling expectations is what's going to get people to visit your little piece of the Internet and keep coming back.

Understanding the expectations of your readers and catering to them is what marketing is all about.

4.2 Web 101

Carving out a space for yourself on the web, while cheaper and easier than most traditional marketing venues, still takes some time and quite a bit of know-how. At the very least, this workbook will prepare you to communicate with a web professional. While I firmly believe that everyone is capable of learning the technical skills necessary to build a web presence, I think that it's a bit like saying that everyone can sing. Sure, with few exceptions, anyone can open their mouth and emit sound, but *should* they?

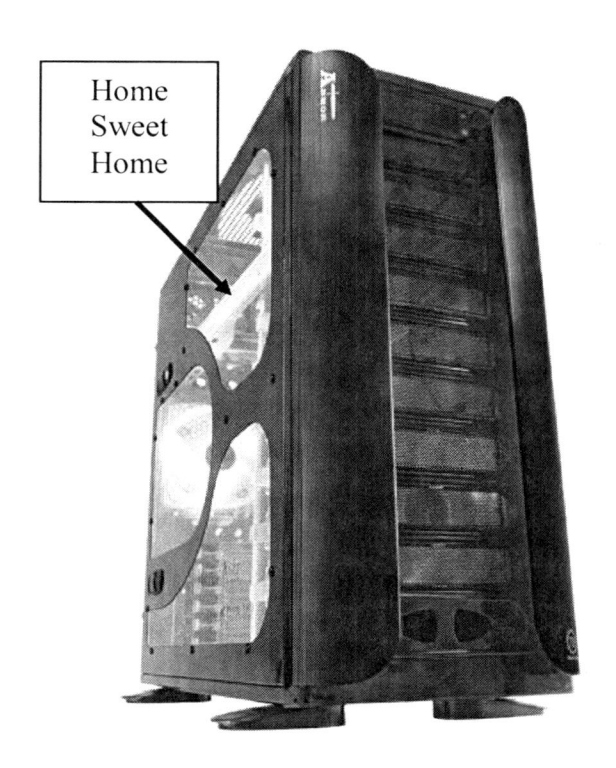

Home Sweet Home

Before going it on your own, consider how much you already know, what skills you already possess, and what your time is worth. Business people are fond of saying that there are three aspects to sales and that you can only ever have two of the three:

1. Cheap
2. Fast
3. Done Well

The "done well" aspect is very important since this is a professional venture on your part. Your web presence needs to reflect that. Here is what you need to know about the Internet.

4.2.1 Hosting and Domains

Your host is the place where the data for your website is going to reside. Essentially, you are going to rent a little website apartment on someone else's high-rise computer complex. You need one.

Your domain name is your web address. Unlike a real apartment building, your website apartment doesn't come with one. You have to choose it and register it with the Internet post office. Your domain name will look something like this: www.writer.org.

That brings us to domain name registry. This can get a bit confusing because, while you can register your domain name through your hosting company, you don't have to. You can register with one company, say Cheap-Domains-R-Us, and then host with another, like Cheap-Hosting-IS-Us.

I highly recommend that you *do not* do this. For sanity's sake, just find one company and do all your business with them. Your hosting company should also provide email addresses using your domain name. It is a lot more professional to have an email address like guru@writer.com than r2-d6@hotmail.com. There are hundreds of domain hosts and registrars out there. I'm going to recommend two: networksolutions.com and godaddy.com.

> **Quick Vocabulary**
>
> Domain Name: Your web address.
>
> ISP: *Internet service provider*; The service that allows you to access the Internet.
>
> Host: The place where your website is located.
>
> Registrar: The place where you purchased your domain name.

I recommend them because they're relatively inexpensive, they're reliable and they have 1-800 numbers you can call and get a person who speaks English on the other end of the line. Network Solutions in particular is a good choice because they own the root servers—the places that all other servers on the Internet look to in order to find each other. If the Internet is an orb web, then Network Solutions is the center point. If they go down, you have bigger problems than getting your email, like surviving nuclear fall-out or running from little green aliens with laser pistols.

Choosing a domain name might seem straightforward, but it can be tricky. We'll go over SEO (*search engine optimization*) in detail in Chapter 5, but I need to mention at this point that when search engines are trying to decide what order to present the websites they know about to a user, the first thing they look at is the domain name.

To illustrate this, go to Google and do a search for "cat." Cat.com is the first listing. Chances are that you weren't expecting the Caterpillar Corporation, but that is who owns cat.com. For this reason, you need to consider what sorts of key phrases people will be searching for when choosing your domain name. Don't let that be the deciding factor—google.com, ebay.com, and amazon.com are cases in point of relevancy not equaling a successful domain name—but at least consider it.

Other things to consider are:

1. Is it meaningful?
2. Does the combination of words spell anything else in the middle?
3. Is it too long to say during a radio interview?
4. Is it too hard to remember?
5. Is it too hard to spell?

Avoid hyphens and underscores in the name. It takes too long to say those things and you absolutely *must* spell out your domain name when talking about it.

I would also try to avoid going with an extension other than .com, .net, or .org. Back in the beginning of the Internet, there was an effort to make the extensions mean something. .com meant a commercial site. .org meant an organization. These days, most organizations also try to own the .com version of their name in addition to any other version that exists. There are a dozen other extensions out there like .us, .info .biz and they will work, but I want you to consider the human brain for a moment.

Pretend that you heard about a great product on a radio show. You were driving at the time and couldn't write down the url, but you remembered the name of the product because it was repeated six times and spelled out for you and the website name was the same as the product. You got home and typed the product name into your web browser. What is the first extension you tried? .com. Second? .org. Third? .net. Failing that, you either resorted to Google, or gave up.

Consider that *human beings* will be typing your domain name into a computer. They misspell things and, unless they have the url on a business card in front of them, they only remember three extensions.

Don't be afraid of owning more than one domain name. Domain names are inexpensive and you don't have to have a different site for each of them. They can all go to the same place. As a starting author with no book, I recommend that you start with some form of your name. As soon as you know the book's title or primary subject matter, purchase that or those as well. Think ahead and be prepared to expand.

There is a fallacy that all the good domain names are already taken. They are not. I managed to purchase my name as late as 2006. What's more, the Internet and domain names have been around long enough for there to be a huge used market for them. You can purchase great domain names at auction, and you get the added benefit of getting all of the residual traffic going to those domains.

Take a few moments and fill out worksheet 4.2.1.

Now that you have your address and rental unit, it's time to think about how to furnish your web apartment.

4.3 Content

There are a few things your web presence should contain in order for it to market you properly. Some mediums are better than others in doing this; in a perfect world you would have multiple Internet venues working together in a cross-promotion bonanza. In this section, I'll offer up a master list. In the next few sections, I'll suggest which type of site might best present your content.

Whether you're published or not, at the absolute minimum there are three things any web presence should contain:

1. A welcome message and statement of purpose
2. Your name and bio
3. A way to contact you

If you filled out worksheet 4.2.1, you will have at least thought about the purpose of your site. I'm going to offer up that the ultimate purpose of your web presence is to sell your work. The purpose you listed on that sheet should be a more streamlined statement, a way to focus your content and dictate the architecture of your site.

What your site needs to do is capture prospect data. A prospect is someone who might be interested in purchasing your book. You'll need to work on the mechanism for doing this as a number one priority.

Worksheet 4.2.1

Domain Names

What is the purpose of the site? _____

_____

_____

If you were looking for the information you plan to present, what words or phrases would you type into a search engine box? _____

_____

_____

_____

If you knew nothing about your topic and needed information on it, what would you type into the keyword box? _____

_____

_____

What is your name? _____

What is the title of your book? _____

Possible Domain Names: _____

_____

_____

_____

_____

_____

_____

Go to www.NetworkSolutions.com and check availability.

You do this by offering a free newsletter, a series of tips or some other incentive. People who want this free information then give you their email address. You deliver on your promise and sneak marketing messages into your email correspondence (more on that in Chapter 6). This is how you begin building your mailing list.

Other content you should offer:

4. A way to capture prospect data
5. A way for people to buy any books you have in print
6. Articles that you've written on your topic

Ideally, you are going to offer more than just the minimum. Remember I mentioned that people on the web had certain expectations? One major expectation is that there will be a lot of free content. Here are some ideas on what that content could be:

7. Excerpts
8. Information about your topic that did not appear in the book (back story, short stories, articles, anecdotes)
9. Reviews
10. News and events about you
11. Audio or video clips
12. Press kits
13. Other books by you
14. Resources and links
15. FAQs (*frequently asked questions*)
16. Any relevant content that someone might find useful

Remember that you are selling yourself as much as your book. Use your imagination and come up with content that presents you and your work in a professional and personable manner. Also, it's a good idea to set yourself up with an affiliate account, such as the ones that Amazon offers (many other online booksellers and e-booksellers have their own, too). Sell your books through your affiliate account and get another 1%. Link any of your resources that happen to be books through your affiliate as well. Use worksheet 4.3 to brainstorm. As you think about your content, consider how that content relates to itself. If you can find groupings, you'll be one step ahead when coming up with a method of presenting it intuitively.

I want to include my standard note on privacy here. Whatever you decide to put up on your website, you need to keep firmly in mind that once it's on the web, it's there for good—even if you change or take your site down. When a search engine, like Google, crawls your site, it makes a copy of it that is stored on the engine's server—usually until the site is crawled again and it's replaced by an update, but not always. There are websites out there whose sole purpose is to archive other websites. I've found copies of my very first attempts at programming—things that I deleted off my local server and even my home computer years ago. Fifteen-year-old data and it's still out there and available to anyone who knows where to look. Thankfully, it's not too embarrassing.

What this means is that you need to think before you put something on the web. You need to find the balance between offering enough information to be personable and accessible, without giving away too much. That goes for any references you might want to include on your site. Ask them before you list them. Don't put their home phone numbers or email addresses up there. I would recommend that you avoid putting up your street address and for goodness sake don't put up your social security number or any personal information about your living family members.

4.4 Websites

A website is a set of interconnected, related resources, prepared and maintained by a person, group, or organization.

Minimally, a website can serve as a 24/7 business card. Better, it can be a brochure, or even a showcase of your work. Even better still, it can do all that plus provide useful information to people, such as articles, how-tos, recipes, instructions, or collections of links and resources. Ideally, it does all this as well as sell your products or services. In essence, it is combination public relations and advertising campaign as well as a storefront, and it's a relatively inexpensive one when compared to other methods of advertising.

A website's strength is that it is persistent. A well structured website provides a stable environment where you can direct people to specific information you want to impart and where people can easily find your product every time they visit.

A website's weakness is also that it is persistent. Your information stays put, so unless you make a point of changing things up, it can become stale. A website is also a bit more difficult to update than other mediums, but it's imperative that you find a way to keep it fresh. A "Quote of the Day" is one way to do this. Another way is to offer up an RSS feed. RSS is *really simple*

Worksheet 4.3
Content

Things I would like my site to contain: _____
_____
_____
_____
_____
_____
_____
_____
_____

Content I already have: _____
_____
_____
_____
_____
_____
_____
_____

Related Content: _____   _____   _____
_____   _____   _____
_____   _____   _____
_____   _____   _____
_____   _____   _____
_____   _____   _____
_____   _____   _____

syndication. You can subscribe to lots of different feeds that will deliver news headlines on any topic you want. Surveys or clever games are other ideas. One clever fiction writer offered up a name generator based on her world.

Because a website is more difficult to update, the methods of keeping the content fresh need to be as automated as you can make them. At the very least, make sure that it's up to date. Announcements of upcoming events need to be replaced with reports of how the event went once they're over. If your email address, phone number, or other contact information changes, update the website. Maybe you've taken the steps necessary to become a speaker. If you're actively pursuing your marketing plan, you will have items on your site that need to change. Change them.

Whenever starting a new website project, it's a good idea to take a few minutes and think about what the site is supposed to be doing for you. Worksheet 4.4 will help you focus.

The type of content that is best served on a website is content that doesn't change very often that includes most of the things I listed under content.

What a website doesn't handle well is news. In fact, even the idea of putting up content that was cut from your book or audio and video clips might not be conducive to a website. Any sort of content that you plan to update on a daily or weekly basis, and present in a chronological order or by topic, is better presented in a blog.

The other thing a website doesn't do well is encourage dialog. An email address and an invitation to contact you are the best a website can offer. As an author, particularly a nonfiction how-to or self-help author, you need to be doing continuous market research. To do that, you must have a method of conversing with your prospects and customers. Blogs can do that to a limited extent via their comment feature, but to really a good old-fashioned heart-to-heart with your prospects, you need a message forum.

4.5 Blogs

Let's start out with the basics. What is a blog? It's a contraction of the words "web" and "log." Harvardlaw.edu describes it as such: "A weblog is a hierarchy of text, images, media objects, and data, arranged chronologically, that can be viewed in an HTML browser." Basically, it's a web-based personal journal about whatever topic the poster wants. It is updated regularly, with content presented in reverse chronological order (newest first).

Worksheet 4.4
Nine Questions

What is the purpose of the site? _____

_____

_____

What is the PRIMARY function of the site? _____

Who is the intended audience? _____

_____

What sort of content is the site to contain? _____

_____

_____

_____

_____

Who will maintain the site after it's launched? _____

Where will the site be hosted? _____

What domain name will you use? _____

Will you need email addresses with your new domain name? _____

How will you monitor your site's effectiveness? _____

_____

_____

Have you looked at any of your competitor's sites? List Them. _____

_____

_____

_____

_____

A blog is just another type of web presence. If you're just starting out and need a site fast, a blog can substitute for a website, though if you're following the plan this workbook is helping you come up with, you will very quickly outgrow it. A blog works best in conjunction with a website.

A blog is more dynamic than a website in that none of its pages remain in the order they were originally put in. It's designed to be updated frequently and to show the most recent updates first, regardless of how you might like to organize that data. There are methods of organization, don't get me wrong, but it is not like a website that has a hierarchy of documents that all stay put. What a blog does best is handle newsy types of things.

As I mentioned earlier, a blog also invites more interaction with its readers through its comment feature. On a website, you have to have a contact box, but that doesn't usually encourage spirited dialog with your visitors.

On that note, a blog is less dynamic and less able to provoke interaction than a forum, but it is also easier to control.

A v-log is just a blog with narcissism. Seriously, it's a blog that includes video clips.

A blog is a serious commitment of time because it needs to be updated frequently. You have to have the discipline to post regularly. Stale blogs do not get readers, and it's readers that you're trying to attract. If you don't commit the time, then your blog won't sustain an audience and is, therefore, probably a waste of time. You have to commit to doing it. No one's going to prod you to post. Avid bloggers update daily.

When considering if a blog is right for you, you must consider if it will take away from time that you could be spending doing something else. There are a few other considerations:

- Do you have something to say?
- Did you want to be the central voice on the site?
- Are you a self-starter?
- Do you like to read? (You need to read what others have written before you post. Reading and responding to other blogs and then linking to them is how you network. It's part of how you get found.)
- Are you thick-skinned? (A blog is a public thing. Even if you restrict who has access to it, it's still on the web and nothing on the web is private. People will comment and not all comments are going to be positive. Sometimes, they're negative just to be mean, with no reason or foundation.)

You're probably wondering how much time we are talking about. Rabid bloggers post daily and sometimes more often than that, but these people don't usually write more than a paragraph or two. For a writer, that's five minutes a post. At that rate, once a day would take less time than deleting the spam in your email box.

I can't seem to get a thought stated in less than 500 words. It takes me a few hours to complete a post so I only ever promised myself a post once a week. Rather than let it languish, I started using it to post my news announcements for easy syndication, archival, and population of my home page. I'm very happy with its performance. I do still post articles to it, but its primary purpose is syndicating press releases.

The two key things are consistency and value. Two paragraph posts are great if you're reporting on daily events or are doing something like the Julie/Julia project (a daily diary of a woman who prepared all 524 recipes in Julia Child's *Mastering the Art of French Cooking, Volume I* in 365 days.) But if you're offering up short stories or full-blown articles, daily posts are just not possible unless you're getting paid to do it.

To make it work you need to be consistent, so pick a plan that you can live with and stick to it. You also need to select a topic that not only promotes your writing, but that has sufficient interest to you to keep posting on it. Worksheet 4.5 will help you come up with some ideas.

You nonfiction authors have a ready-made topic in your book. Why not blog about it so that every post generates interest and community and provides the opportunity for comment and research?

For you fiction writers, here are a few examples of what other fiction writers have done. First, there's me. Despite what you may think in reading this workbook, I consider myself a fiction writer. Fiction is my passion. Historical fiction, fantasy, romance, science fiction, and any cross-genre combination thereof is what fills my head until it hurts and I have to write the stories down. I have a historical novel in print, I'm shopping a fantasy allegory and I'm drafting a science fiction romance novel. My blog is on my day job: Internet marketing and web development.

I found a blog for another science fiction writer who blogs about science fiction, current events, web programming, and writing. Many of the writers' resource blogs on the web are run by fiction writers. Their topic is the writing process in some form or another. Other fiction writers review other books in their genre, or report on events happening at genre clubs, events, and meetings.

4.5.1 Blogging Platforms

Now that we have a handle on the what, let's look at the how. A platform, when the term is used in reference to blogs, is the software package that's going to make your blog run. I'm going to go over two of the most popular free ones out there, but there are many paid hosting platforms available that are also very good. Typically, the paid or self-hosted platforms are going to be the most customizable. I've listed some of the more popular ones in the resources list at the back of the book.

With my two favorite freebies, Blogger and WordPress, you are given a domain name that looks something like this: marketingwebdesign.wordpress.com. Both platforms also allow you to use your own domain name while still hosting on their system. WordPress charges $15 a year for hosting the domain name and you have to register your domain name with NetworkSolutions or some other registrar. Blogger will host it for free. For $10 a year, you can register through Blogger and avoid another registrar completely. Wordpress will allow you to modify their templates for a small fee as well, but you'd better know what you're doing before you attempt anything fancy.

Worksheet 4.5
Blogging Topics

What do I want my blog to do for me? _____

_____

What do I know a lot about? _____

_____

_____

_____

_____

_____

_____

What do I like to read? _____

_____

_____

_____

_____

How does what I know and what I read relate to what I want my blog to do?

_____

_____

_____

Notes: _____

_____

_____

_____

Let's start with whether you should host the software yourself or use a hosted platform. It really comes down to how customized you want your blog to be. Here are a few comparisons:

1 Hosted Platforms	2 Stand-Alone Platforms
Many Free Options	Must Pay for Hosting of Domain Name
Fast, Easy Set-up	More Difficult Set-up
Less Control of Look and Feel	More Control of Look and Feel
Automatic Software Updates	You Update Software
Quick Indexing by Search Engines	Slower Indexing

Now let's set up a blog using a free hosting package and you can see what I mean about fast and easy.

1. Create Free Account.

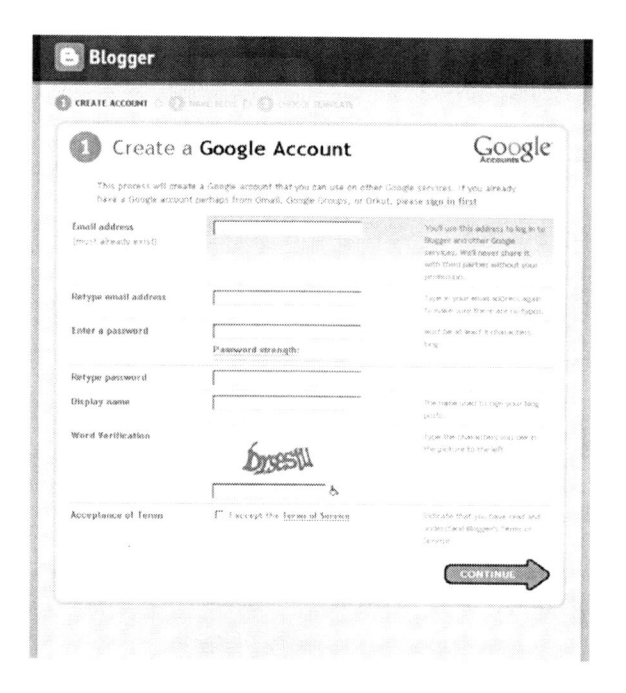

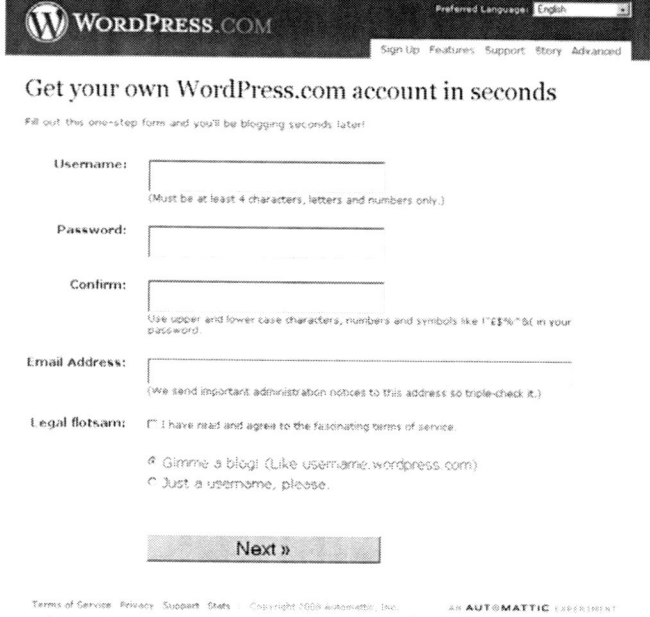

Angela Render

2. Choose name and url for blog.

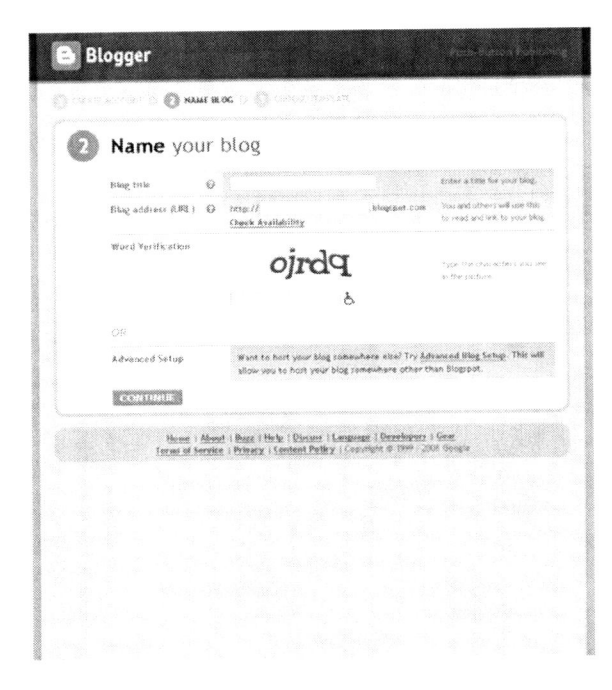

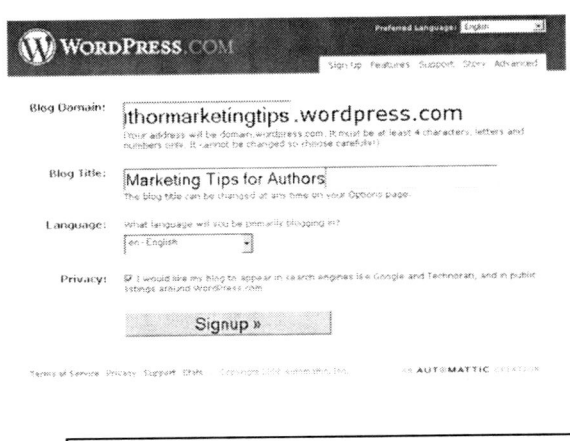

(Blogger lets you use a custom domain name here. Or change to a custom url later. Wordpress has another page after you get set up.)

3. Choose a template

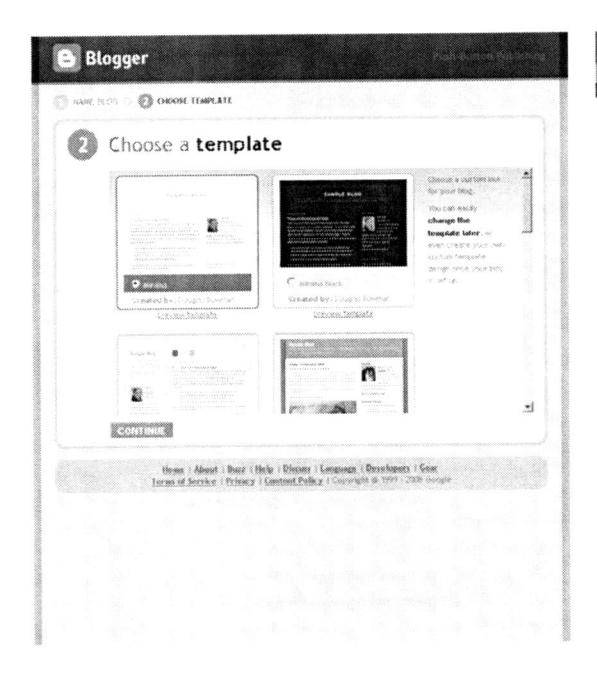

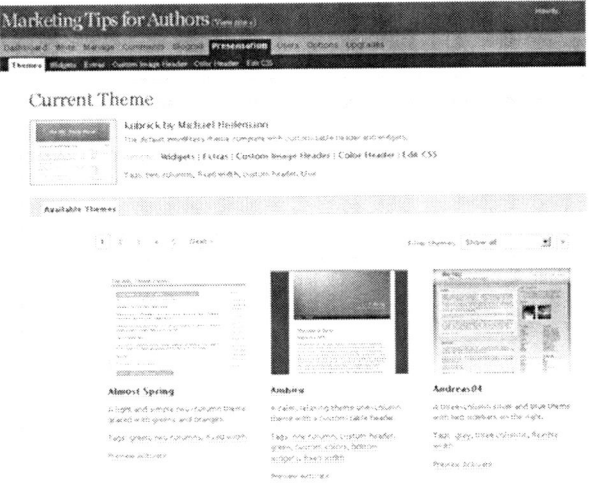

(Blogger has six or so to choose from, but they are very customizable. Wordpress has something like 30, but you have to be careful which ones you pick because some are very flexible and others are not at all.)

4. Start Posting

That wasn't such a chore, now was it?

4.5.2 Posting Tips

People on the web are looking for one of four things:

- Entertainment
- Information
- Community
- Shopping

You don't have to present original content on your blog, but make sure what you present is unique and in your own voice. Recycle passages from your own published works. Just re-word them a bit.

Don't plagiarize. The same rules here apply as to any other form of writing. Quote, give proper credit, analyze, re-structure, and criticize. There's plenty of perspective to go around.

Posts can be any length, so long as they're providing something of value to the reader. Refer to the four reasons mentioned above to determine why they might have come to visit you.

> "If you steal one person's work, you're a plagiarist. If you steal everyone's work, you're a researcher."
>
> —Matthew Bennett

For longer posts, make sure to break up the text with white space, subheads, bulleted lists, images or even multiple pages. Internet surfers treat a thick block of text like a two story cinderblock wall. They encounter it, size it up, and go around. The same block of text in print wouldn't phase them. It's the backlit screen you need to overcome. Keep paragraphs short with friendly white space between them.

On that note, when you pick your blog colors, be mindful of your readers. Dark backgrounds with light text can be very dramatic. They're also hard on the eye. Some blogs can get away with it if they have lots of pictures with very little text. Do not put a pattern behind your text. You can't always trust the templates these blogging packages offer either. Use your own good judgment.

Keep each post focused on a narrow aspect of your topic and don't ramble. You need to pace yourself anyway if you want to have something to talk about over the long haul so don't dump all your knowledge into a single, rambling post.

- Put any keywords in your text body in a bold or italic font so readers scanning for them can find them. Better yet, pull them out as subheads
- Use bullet points
- Make lists to highlight your key points
- Present your conclusion in the first paragraph rather than building toward it and burying it in the last paragraph
- Put boxes around key points to draw attention to them
- Think of your blog titles as mini newspaper headlines. By default, headlines tend to have keywords in them. They're also punchy and designed to generate interest in the article.
- Link back to previous posts you've written
- Use pull-quotes and call-outs
- Quote yourself
- Quote others and link to them
- Use colors
- Include audio or video clips
- Images
- Interview people
- Have guest bloggers or take on partners
- Invite interactivity through polls and assignments, and ask for comments
- Write posts in series to draw readers back

As I mentioned before, it's important that you do *not* put personal information in your posts. I found a forum where its mommy members were posting full names, dates of birth, and places of residence for their kids along with pictures and it wasn't even password protected. No, no, no! Once information is on the web, it's there for good. Think before you post.

4.6 Forums

A forum is a message board with many topics (threads) of discussion related to a common topic. Forums are a great way to create community on the web. Regular posters get to know each other and consider each other friends. A forum encourages dialog and dialog between author and reader is essential to good marketing.

Before you run out and start up a forum, there are a couple of drawbacks you should consider. First is that the topics of discussion can be initiated by anyone subscribing to the forum and for that reason, a forum is harder to control than a blog. There's moderation and spam control, but if you get the reputation of being heavy-handed people will stop posting. Freedom of speech, remember?

The other point is a logistics issue. In order for a forum to attract people and keep them coming back, it has to be busy. To be busy it has to have a lot of people posting frequently. There's the problem with starting a forum of your own. Unless you already have traffic, you can't generate it.

I advise my clients to hold off on creating a forum until they have a mass of people already interested in them and the topic. I recommend starting with a blog and with creating a list of potentially interested parties from your in-person gigs. Once you have an established, well-trafficked blog, enlist the help of five chatty friends—offer them pizza parties if you have to. Now you're ready to create a forum.

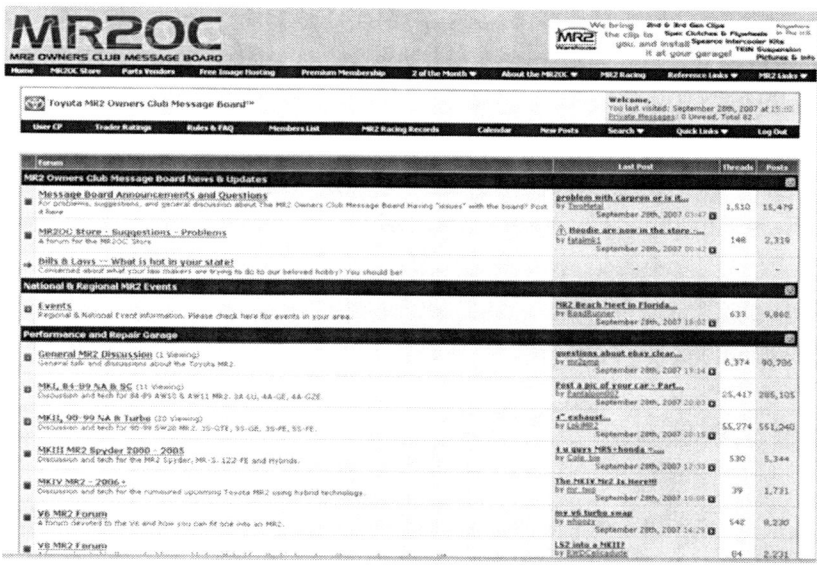

Until then, prowl established forums on your topic or on topics related to yours. Become a regular friend and valued member of that community. Check out Twitter or some other open chat site. You can promote your own site or blog on the forum through your byline. Then, when you start your own forum, you can invite your new friends to join.

4.7 Audio and Visual Media

There is nothing in the world that can replace an in-person meeting with someone in terms of making a lasting impression as well as a bond with that person. There's a reason that political candidates still do small-town appearances and debates. Television alone isn't enough. The problem is that, unless you're booking to crowds of 100,000, or spend all of your time traveling and attending events, it's physically impossible to make that sort of connection with the volume of people you need to reach.

The next best thing is a video recording on the web. Through a video, people can see and hear you. They can read your facial expressions and mannerisms and feel as if they know you better. The written word can be interpreted very differently by different people. A phrase meant as a joke can come off offensive in print, but would be funny if the audience could see you deliver it.

After video comes audio. Hearing your voice, the inflections and the undertones can create another level of intimacy that would be missing in print alone.

Is there anyone reading this who has not visited YouTube? YouTube is the epitome of a successful video site. If you're not quite ready for prime-time video, there are methods of posting and syndicating audio files, which I'll go over below. If you don't want to get in front of the camera, create your own book trailers and post them.

4.7.1 Podcasts

A podcast is an electronic audio recording that you can post on your website or blog. The term came from Apple's iPod, but it has come to mean any audio format. Mp3 is the most commonly recognized format. With some very simple software and a microphone, you can digitally record yourself reading some of your work. Think of it as an audio postcard advertisement. Mention your url at the beginning and end and invite people to visit your site for more information or recordings, or whatever you're offering. Podcasts lend themselves very nicely to RSS feeds and there are even established venues that will accept your submissions and then syndicate them. Podcast.net and podcast.com are both free places where you can post your podcasts. Podcast.com even has its own blog with instructions on how to get started at blog.podcast.com.

Audio recordings of excerpts of your work can be burned onto CDs and distributed at book fairs, readings, or speaking engagements. Offer one as an incentive to purchase now at your next signing. Be creative: just make sure you include your web address on the recording.

4.7.2 Book Trailers

Book trailers are rapidly growing in popularity. HarperCollins is even on board and offers trailers for some of their titles on their website. Circle of Seven Productions trademarked the term in 2002. A book trailer is like a movie trailer: a one to three minute audio/video production advertising your book. Reducing a 400 page novel to a three minute sensory bonanza is a daunting task, but there are companies eager to perform it for you. A book trailer can be as simple as a video of the author reading, or as elaborate as a movie trailer.

As expensive to produce as they are, they are handy to have. You can distribute them on the Internet. You can offer them as a clip to play during a television interview. Use them as an intro for your next speaking engagement or book signing. Burn them onto DVDs and offer them as an incentive to buy your book today.

4.7.3 Video

You can easily create and post videos of yourself giving readings or even talking about the post you're putting up. Windows comes with a program called Windows Video Maker that will capture most anything you want. Purchase a webcam, install it and play. YouTube has instructional videos to watch under their "help" menu.

Programs like Fraps can record what's happening on your screen, so if you're blogging about video games or something else that's happening on your computer, you can include clips or how-to demos. Citrix's GoTo Meeting will do that as well as allow you to have an audience. You can marry a PowerPoint presentation to a voice recording this way.

4.8 Design

Now that you've done all this, you're ready to start designing. Let's take a couple of moments here and go over common vocabulary so you can speak with a designer and know what they're saying.

1. **Home Page** – the first page people see when they type in your url.
2. **Header** – This tells the person who clicked on a link where they are. This needs to be persistent across your site.
3. **Navigation** – the links to get from one page of your site to the next. This can appear just under the header, horizontally, or along either the left or right sides of the page. This too needs to be persistent or your visitors can become lost. The caveat here is for really big sites that have lots of easily categorized pages. These sites will sometimes have the main navigation across the top and then category specific navigation along the side.
4. **Footer** – The section along the bottom of the web page. This will have a copyright notice, design credit, and possibly a repeat of some

of the more important navigation elements, or some less used elements like privacy statements.
5. **Callout** – Something you want attention brought to. These don't necessarily have to appear on the home page.
6. **Sub Page** – The pages reached by the top level of navigation. Sometimes called "category page." For some of you, this may be as far as any of it goes. These pages typically have a different organization to them than the home page.
7. **Sub Header** – Sub page title
8. **Sub-sub Page** – Any page organized below a sub page.
9. **Breadcrumb** – A trail of links so that the person knows at a glance where they are on your site.

What should your site look like? Form follows function. Now that you've identified the function, you can start looking around at colors and designs that will best highlight your work.

Your website possibilities are in two categories: template and custom. Template sites use someone else's artistic vision. You just fill in the content. Network Solutions and GoDaddy both offer free templates for you to use to build your site. I can't speak for GoDaddy, but I've seen Network Solutions's offerings. There are maybe eight models to choose from and you absolutely do NOT do any sort of customization. ISPs are getting in on the act and one of my students recommended Comcast's templates. I am definitely interested in reviews on the various template offerings, so if you have something to contribute, please comment on my blog entry: www.angelarender.com/internetmarketingtips/2008/08/website-template-software-what-is-your-favorite-package

For a monthly fee, GoDaddy says they will create and maintain a custom site for you. I have no reports on this service.

There are places on the web that offer design templates for free or for a fee. They can be quite attractive and professional looking. They can be very cost effective, but some templates can cost $800 and up. There are hundreds of these, but there is always the chance you'll encounter someone else's site that looks just like yours.

Also keep in mind that it's the design and skeleton you are purchasing. To put your content in them, you need to either learn HTML coding or some of them will work with Dreamweaver or FrontPage. Those are two applications

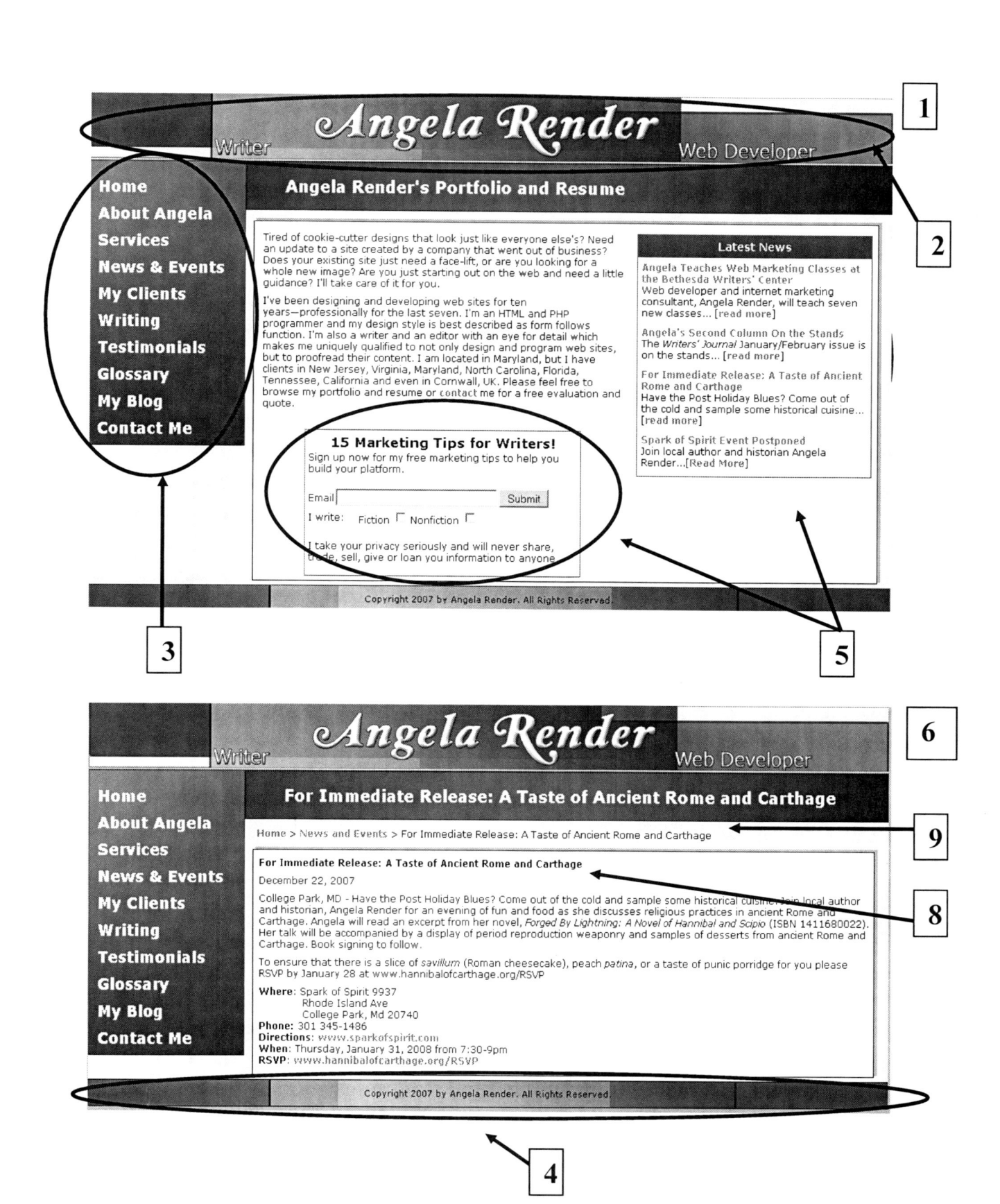

Marketing for Writers

Screenshot 1: Angela Render's Portfolio and Resume

[1] Header banner with "Angela Render" logo, "Writer" on left and "Web Developer" on right (circled).

[2] Right edge of header area.

[3] Left navigation menu (circled):
- Home
- About Angela
- Services
- News & Events
- My Clients
- Writing
- Testimonials
- Glossary
- My Blog
- Contact Me

Angela Render's Portfolio and Resume

Tired of cookie-cutter designs that look just like everyone else's? Need an update to a site created by a company that went out of business? Does your existing site just need a face-lift, or are you looking for a whole new image? Are you just starting out on the web and need a little guidance? I'll take care of it for you.

I've been designing and developing web sites for ten years—professionally for the last seven. I'm an HTML and PHP programmer and my design style is best described as form follows function. I'm also a writer and an editor with an eye for detail which makes me uniquely qualified to not only design and program web sites, but to proofread their content. I am located in Maryland, but I have clients in New Jersey, Virginia, Maryland, North Carolina, Florida, Tennessee, California and even in Cornwall, UK. Please feel free to browse my portfolio and resume or contact me for a free evaluation and quote.

15 Marketing Tips for Writers!
Sign up now for my free marketing tips to help you build your platform.

Email [_____] [Submit]
I write: Fiction ☐ Nonfiction ☐

I take your privacy seriously and will never share, trade, sell, give or loan you information to anyone.

Latest News

Angela Teaches Web Marketing Classes at the Bethesda Writers' Center
Web developer and internet marketing consultant, Angela Render, will teach seven new classes... [read more]

Angela's Second Column On the Stands
The *Writers' Journal* January/February issue is on the stands... [read more]

For Immediate Release: A Taste of Ancient Rome and Carthage
Have the Post Holiday Blues? Come out of the cold and sample some historical cuisine... [read more]

Spark of Spirit Event Postponed
Join local author and historian Angela Render...[Read More]

Copyright 2007 by Angela Render. All Rights Reserved.

[5] Arrows pointing to the "15 Marketing Tips for Writers!" sign-up form and the Latest News sidebar.

Screenshot 2: For Immediate Release page

[6] Header banner.

For Immediate Release: A Taste of Ancient Rome and Carthage

[9] Home > News and Events > For Immediate Release: A Taste of Ancient Rome and Carthage

[8] For Immediate Release: A Taste of Ancient Rome and Carthage
December 22, 2007

College Park, MD - Have the Post Holiday Blues? Come out of the cold and sample some historical cuisine. Join local author and historian, Angela Render for an evening of fun and food as she discusses religious practices in ancient Rome and Carthage. Angela will read an excerpt from her novel, *Forged By Lightning: A Novel of Hannibal and Scipio* (ISBN 1411680022). Her talk will be accompanied by a display of period reproduction weaponry and samples of desserts from ancient Rome and Carthage. Book signing to follow.

To ensure that there is a slice of *savillum* (Roman cheesecake), peach *patina*, or a taste of punic porridge for you please RSVP by January 28 at www.hannibalofcarthage.org/RSVP

Where: Spark of Spirit 9937
Rhode Island Ave
College Park, Md 20740
Phone: 301 345-1486
Directions: www.sparkofspirit.com
When: Thursday, January 31, 2008 from 7:30-9pm
RSVP: www.hannibalofcarthage.org/RSVP

Copyright 2007 by Angela Render. All Rights Reserved.

[4] Arrow pointing to footer bar (circled).

that allow you to do WYSIWYG (what you see is what you get) drag-and-drop web design. Or you need to hire or shanghai a web programmer to do it for you.

A custom site is one that is designed and programmed just for you. Some programmers can put in an easy way for you to update your content, but you'll probably need to go back to them to create a new page. With a custom site, there's no issue with the font or color. You have your own personal touches in them so you can effectively brand yourself with your site.

> **Quick Vocabulary**
>
> Web Designer: An artist who will design a graphically beautiful website. They may or may not program it for you.
>
> Web Programmer: Computer programmer who may or may not be able to design a site.
>
> Web Developer: Hybrid designer and programmer.

If you decide to look for help, there are three basic types of web people out there.

Graphics designers (aka web designers) are usually artists. They are great for beautiful design work. They may or may not be able to program the site for you. Their designs can cost in the low hundreds to a thousand depending on the complexity. If they're Flash programmers, they may try and do the site for you in flash. Don't let that happen. Flash is awesome for what it does, but inappropriate for an entire site—or even the navigation of a site to be in. In the end, you'll be in the same position as you would have been with the templates and need to find a programmer or a developer to get the site up and running.

A note on Flash. Flash is a program developed by Macromedia (now owned by Adobe) that allows the creation of animated or interactive features. Flash is a movie. As such, it has some strengths and weaknesses that you should be aware of. Flash at its best can be a full, interactive tutorial, a video game or an animated comic book. Flash also makes great moving headers for sites, or animated advertisements. Flash can and has been used for scrolling navigation or even for a complete website including the text. The weakness is that Flash is a picture. Flash text is fuzzy and cannot be read by people using readers (i.e. the blind) or, with the exception of links, by search engine crawlers. For this reason, you should not use Flash for your navigation or for the body of your site. Doing so makes it inaccessible to the blind and impossible for search engines to properly index. Also, unless you are a Flash programmer, editing the site is costly and time consuming.

Web programmers do what their title suggests. They program sites. They are going to be heavy on the technological side and light on the graphics design side. Their services fall in about the same price range as the designers. If you need a complex form or a calculator or something cool on your site, these are the guys to go to. They make it happen.

Web developers are hybrids. Depending on the person, they will be better in the design or in the programming area, but they are comfortable doing both and can be a good choice for one-stop-shopping.

When choosing, it's important to feel comfortable with the person you plan on working with. It doesn't matter how good the programmer or designer is if you can't communicate your ideas.

4.8.1 Programming for Accessibility

It's a good idea to program your site to be hospitable to the visually impaired. If your target market is aging or suffering from a vision-reducing infirmity, it's essential. After studying your market, you may discover that a large portion of your potential audience is visually impaired. The Web Accessibility Initiative has a lot of information on this subject. Your web developer should know most of this, but programming for accessibility takes some planning and know-how. It's important to at least mention it up front when discussing your project. I want to provide a bit of guidance so that you know how to discuss it.

The visually impaired use readers and keystrokes to navigate the web. These readers get hung up with javascript and with Flash. A reader cannot read the content displayed in an image either. Avoid presenting your content in these ways. If you find you need a drop-down menu or something cool to happen when you scroll over an image or text, CSS is your new best friend.

> **Quick Vocabulary**
>
> CSS: (*cascading style sheet*) a way of rendering the look and behavior of a web page

4.9 Traffic Tracking

Website statistics will help you keep track of how popular your website is and how well your Internet marketing campaign is performing. There are a bunch of tracking services out there. WebTrends is a big one. There is also a fantastic open source code package available called Analog. Alexa.com is a service that makes your traffic viewable to everyone, including the public. NetworkSolutions and GoDaddy offer web tracking software as part of their service and I imagine there are other services out there that do the same. If you install a link of javascript code on your site, Google Analytics will analyze your traffic data as well.

The tracking packages that do not rely on a script all rely on your server's log files, which more and more hosting companies are not offering, or are only keeping for a month at a time. Just so you know, everything that happens on the web is recorded. Each time you try to visit a website, your ISP records the request, Network Solutions records the request from your ISP, and the server with the data records the request. Then the delivery is recorded all the way back. Starting to feel paranoid? Those records are called log files. Analytics software takes the raw log files and runs them through filters so you can read the data in a useful format.

The big thing about reading these is knowing what the numbers mean, so I'm going to give you a few more vocabulary words:

1. **Hits** – the biggest number you're going to see. Hits include ALL files requested. Every image, every include and every page counts as a hit so one "page view" may be equal to 10-80 hits. The number is big and gratifying and utterly useless. Some software packages don't even report hits anymore.
2. **Page Views** – the total number of pages viewed on your site. Much more useful. Basically the image requests and other things have been filtered out.
3. **Unique Visit or Unique Page View** – filters out multiple requests for the same page from the same requesting server.
4. **Referrer** – The server that delivered your viewer to your site.

Keep in mind that all of this data can be skewed by the way some aspects of the web work. This is where Google Analytics can do a better job than the raw log files, because that line of code will report to Google exactly who requested the page. Sometimes. Google Analytics can be fooled as well. Anyone who has javascript disabled or who is running a privacy screening program will block Google Analytics.

If you want to get a real handle on how you're doing, use both and compare them. Even then, your traffic statistics are best used when compared month to month over time.

This data is useful on a book proposal because a stream of monthly page views that consistently increases each month indicates a strong web presence. That's advertising for the book. The data is also useful for you to analyze what information on your site is popular and what isn't. Some packages will track how a person navigates your site and can pinpoint flaws in the architecture, or pages that are missing.

These programs will also tell you cool stuff like what web browsers people are using (you must program so it looks good in both Firefox *and* Internet Explorer), where the visitor came from (was it a link off a site or from a search engine?), if they requested mp3s or PDFs, how long they stayed, even what country they're from. All sorts of stuff.

4.10 Copyrights and Images

The number one question asked of me about writing and the web is, "Is my work copyrighted?" In 2001, the US Supreme Court said that reprinting newspaper or magazine articles on the web without permission violated US copyright law. So yes, the same copyright laws that are there for print also apply to the web—provided that you enforce your rights. If a copyright notice is not present on a page, it does not necessarily mean that the author has waived their rights.

A quick word on "netiquette." All quoting rules apply here as with the printed word. The one addition is that you should link back to the original source of your quote whenever possible. If you want to make other authors happy, quote them with proper attributes and then provide links to their sites as a great resource for more information. You want links to your work as well. Linking is what makes the web a web.

What's different about the Internet and copyright is that it's so much easier to lift text and images off of the electronic media and reuse it, and the volume is so great that there's a good chance no one will ever know. So when it comes to your writing, assume that it is now effectively public domain as soon as you post it on the web and you'll never be disappointed.

This is something for you to keep in mind about using pictures you've found on the web. Same thing applies: if the photographer has not expressly given permission to use the image, you must assume it is under copyright. So if you find a great picture on the web that would be just perfect to illustrate your article, you need to contact the owner and get permission. There are rights-free images out there. I've put a list of some of the places you can look for them in the resources list. There are more out there and I welcome emails letting me know of great new resources.

If you decide to be your own photographer, you need to keep in mind that you can't just post any picture you've taken. Pictures taken in public places, especially if they've focused in on someone specific, have certain rules attached to them. The law is on the side of the photographed subject if they have a "reasonable expectation of privacy." Public events are probably okay as long as they are general crowd shots or of a performer. But this isn't necessarily always the case. Remember recently Google got in trouble for taking street-level photographs for the "street view" option on their map service? Look now and you can see that all of the images are just blurry enough so that you can't make out facial features or license plates. There are areas of the country that will never have this feature because there are too many government buildings.

If you're in a private venue, and a restaurant with a performer *is* a private venue, ask first. Especially be careful when taking pictures of minors. To cover yourself, carry a few consent forms in your purse or camera bag. I've included a sample photo release for you. Talk to your photo subjects. Tell them what it's for and get written permission to use it. Promise to email a copy of the picture. Make a new friend and potentially a loyal reader.

4.10.1 Protecting Your Copyright

Now that you're paranoid about someone stealing your work, let me reassure you that the same amount of paranoia greeted the photocopy machine when its use became widespread. For a determined individual, any published work can be stolen. It might take them re-typing it, but they'll get it if they really want it. The same holds true for images.

There are a few things you can tell your developer to do that will make getting your work difficult enough to dissuade casual swiping. For text, the best safe way to present it is in a PDF (*portable document file*) format. A PDF behaves like a picture in that you can't just highlight the text, copy it, and paste it somewhere else. A PDF is also readable by search engine crawlers so protecting your work doesn't automatically exclude that beautiful content from your ranking scale.

Another way to handle text is in a Flash movie. The Flash movie has the same safety mechanism a PDF has, but there are a couple of drawbacks. First off, search engines can't read it, so all of that valuable content is invisible to them. The second drawback is updating the text. If you find an error in it or want to add to it later, you have to find a Flash programmer to do it for you. A PDF is easier. Just open the original file, make the changes and save it out as a PDF again.

For images, the best way to dissuade copying is to embed a watermark in it. The drawback is that your lovely image has what amounts to a tattoo on it. Another method is to run a javascript that prevents people from right-clicking on the images. The drawback to this is that if people are blocking javascript, it doesn't work. Flash movies work as well to prevent easy downloading, but editing the movie poses the same difficulty as editing the text.

Having said that, Flash is a fantastic choice for graphic novels. A good programmer can make the pages turn and put in all sorts of cool effects. The warning I give you is that Flash programmers are prohibitively expensive. You graphic novelists should consider learning to program it yourself.

4.10.2 Image Editing

The best practice for images in general is to crop the image down to exactly the size you need it to be and present it as a 72dpi .jpg. If the image is too small, or not high enough resolution, a potential image stealer might pass it up and look for someone else's.

Standard image sizes (in pixels)
- 75x75
- 100x100
- 250x179
- 400x286

The trick to getting an image to lay out correctly with text around it, like in a in a blog post, or in the middle of a page is to mind the width. 250px will make an image large enough to be recognizable, yet small enough to have the text wrap around it comfortably. A panoramic shot or an enlargement would be 450-550px. Let the height take care of itself.

When presenting a series of images in a gallery format, the trick to getting it to look good from shot to shot is to make all of the heights the same and let the width fluctuate. 300-450px is a good height for an image gallery.

For those of you with the money and time to invest in a robust graphics design program, Adobe Photoshop is extremely powerful and can do most anything you want. It is a professional quality program, though, and it takes practice to make it work for you. I recommend *Photoshop Wow!* By Linnea Dayton and Cristen Gillespie. It'll teach you how to make the most of Photoshop.

Angela Render

For those of you who only need basic photo editing, I found an amazing free program that will let you crop, color correct, resize, and fix red-eye. Pho.to is easy to use and gets the job done.

PhotoRelease

I, (please print your name) _____,

Give _____, the absolute right and permission to use my image taken today. I understand that the photographs may be used in a publication, electronic media (e.g., video, CD ROM, Internet/WWW), or other form of publication or promotion.

I release _____, the photographer, their offices, employees, agents, and designees from liability for any violation of any personal or proprietary right I may have in connection with such use. I am 18 years of age or older.

Signature _____

Address _____

City _____ State _____

Zip _____

Email _____

Phone (_____) _____

Date _____

☐ Please let me know when and where I can view my image.

Chapter 5

Getting Found

5.1 The Secrets of SEO

Since the Internet is one of the least expensive ways of marketing yourself, it's important that people be able to find your web presence. SEO (*search engine optimization*) is a buzz-word among web development companies and marketing firms. They offer high-priced analyses and optimization solutions and blah, blah, blah. The fact of the matter is that you can do most of this yourself, provided that you remember a few key principals, think things through, come up with a plan, and then actually execute it.

Search engine optimization is the art of making your web presence easily readable and highly attractive to search engines like Google, Live Search, Ask, Yahoo, etc. It is important that you look good to them because you need to have your web pages place highly in their search results.

> **Quick Vocabulary**
>
> Organic Search: Free search placement

How many people here, when searching for something on the web, click-through to the second page of listings? The third? My point exactly. You either find what you're looking for on the first page or you type in a slightly different search and try again.

That means that your pages need to rank in the top 10 for them to get a fighting chance of being seen through organic search. The closer to number 1 you can get, the better.

Organic search is the free search rankings. You can also pay to have your link appear at the top of the generated list. I'll go into paid search a bit later. I want to focus on organic for now because SEO refers specifically to the organic placement of your site. If you're going to pay for your placement, you can ignore SEO, but you probably shouldn't ignore all of it. Good SEO formatting requires many of the same things that make for an effective site in general.

Search engines, despite what everyone thinks, have not been around since the birth of the web. Rather, they sprang out of a need to find things after the web had been around a while. Google has only been around since the late 1990s. The web has been around since the 1980s. Back BG (before Google) you started with links from your ISP and then manually clicked your way through pages of links until you found what you were looking for.

Google, and its predecessors, changed all that by writing programs that would click through all those links for you ahead of time, index them based on content and then present them to anyone who typed a query into their search box. These programs are called web crawlers and they spider their way through the links on the web.

To help the crawlers, meta tags were added to the web programming language. These tags are an opportunity for website owners to give the crawlers a quick overview of what is on their sites. With the exception of the title and description meta tags, this data is not seen by human eyeballs. The tags are embedded in the header code of your site.

```
<HEAD>
<TITLE>Title of your site</TITLE>
<meta name="description" content="What your site is about.">
<meta name="keywords" content="relevant words, or, phrases">
</HEAD>
```

Then unscrupulous businesses (dare I mention the porn industry?) took advantage of the lack of human supervision and started cheating—trying to trick the crawlers into offering up their sites as top results for keyword searches totally unrelated to their content.

The programmers countered with savvier ranking criteria. The actual formulas used for determining relevancy are constantly changing and are heavily guarded secrets, but you weren't interested in tricking the crawlers anyway, right? You really have something of value to offer and people deserve the privilege of seeing it.

Despite the shifting algorithms, there are a few things that remain constant and indisputable in getting good organic search placement:

- Relevant content
- Effective formatting
- Useful or unique page titles
- Links
- Meta tag keywording (Blog version = topic keywording)
- Longevity

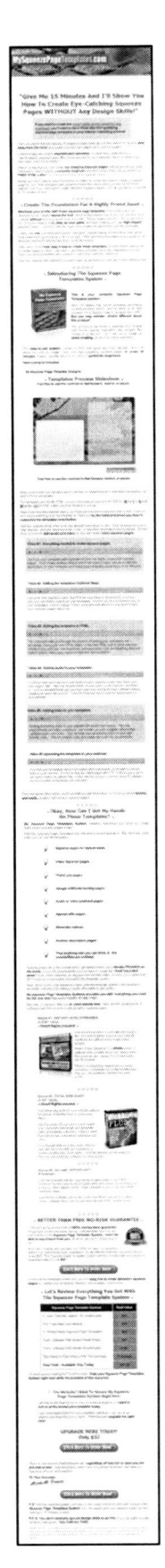

Some of these are completely dependent on you. Some you might have to hire programmers for. Let's start with what you can and must be responsible for yourself.

5.1.1 Relevant Content

If you read and remember my history lesson from Chapter 4, then you know that people searching the web come to it with certain expectations. Web crawlers are programmed with those expectations behind them. Commerce and entertainment are latecomers to the web. Content has always been the foundation of the web and it is still the most valuable tool you have in getting your pages found. More content = better placement. Fresh content = even better placement and crawlers that visit more often.

Writers have a definite edge over others because writing is a powerful skill. You have a lot to say and you are capable of saying it well, so the "good" and "content" parts are easy. It's the "relevant" that may elude you. For that reason, you need to have a firm grasp of what you're trying to present and make sure you keep your focus.

5.1.2 Effective Formatting

This can be tricky because crawlers count how many times the keyword in question has been used on your page and whether the keywords in your meta tags are consistent with the data. That's why some of the older squeeze pages rank so highly, despite the fact that no human being would ever actually read the whole thing.

A squeeze page is a web page whose sole purpose is to get you to buy something or sign up for something. Some are hour-long infomercials on a page. There's a little information and a lot of "buy now."

Crawlers love this sort of thing because it appears to have a ton of content all in one page, no cheating. There is a tiny example of one running down the left side of the page. Would any of you read all this? I wouldn't.

Humans like to read something more like what's on the next page.

This is a tad long, but formatted in such a way as to not be intimidating. Let's take a moment and look at what he's done right. (By the way, if you're looking for prime examples of how to format your content for both blogs and web pages, check out problogger.com. Darren Rowse, the ProBlogger himself, both preaches it and practices it.)

If you've taken a class on formatting for any sort of writing, then you know that modern web searchers will not read densely presented pages. Notice here:

- One and two sentence paragraphs
- Lots of white space
- Clear, bold subheads
- Lists and bullet points

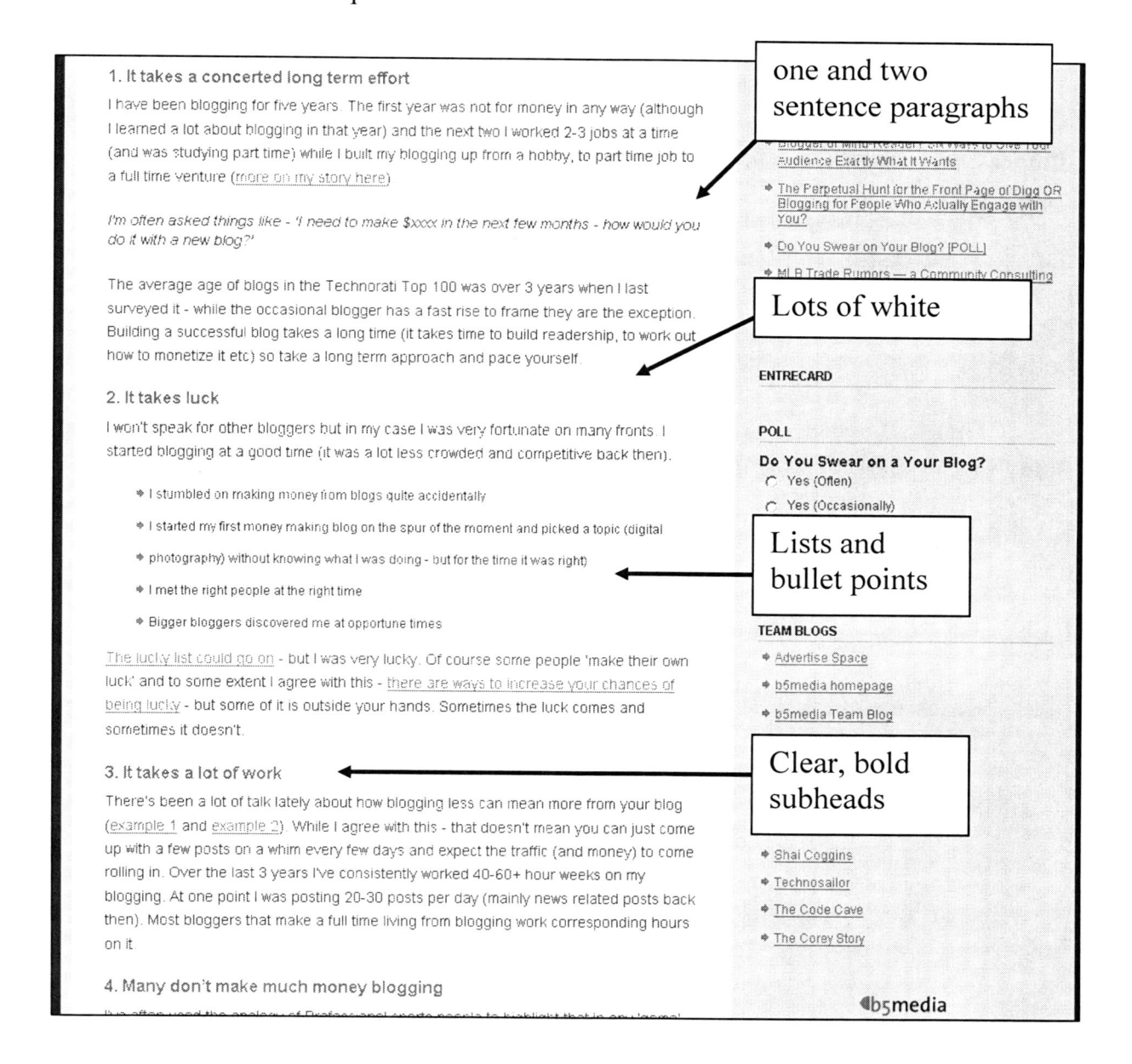

These are all things that make the text easier on the eye, and therefore more likely to be read. Images, pull-quotes, and boxed sidebars are other effective ways of breaking up the page.

5.1.3 Useful or Unique Page Titles

Which type you need will depend on whether you're talking about a website or a blog. "Useful" goes with website. Useful page titles tell the user where they are. For example, my website page titles look like: Angela Render Web Design – About Me, or Angela Render Web Design – My Clients. No matter what page you're on, you know that you're on my site and which page on my site you're looking at. Ideally, page titles will be relevant to the content on the page. By the way, both the site and page title need to also appear in the meta data title tag. People who are visually impaired and use readers will benefit from good titles as well.

"Unique" is more for blog entries. Treat each title like a mini headline. Make it exciting and full of keywords, or phrase it as a question that mirrors the question people might ask about your topic.

The reason page titles are so important is because crawlers still assume that your headings will be indicative of the type of content on the page. In order to make them appear larger and bolder, the coding uses certain common tags. The crawlers look for these specifically and weight the text between them more heavily.

Thanks to cascading style sheets (*CSS*), programmers are able to override many of the defaults and make the tags look like anything we want them to.

5.1.4 Links

Links are what makes the web the web. After content, they are the most important thing you can have on your site. They are also the most tricky.

> **Quick Vocabulary**
>
> Embedded Links: Clickable words or phrases in the body of the text on a web page.

There are three types of links. The first includes links between pages on your own website. This would include navigation links as well as embedded links to more information on the subject. For blogs this is mandatory, especially if you've previously made a point on the same subject, or one article builds off of another. This would also include links from blog postings to your web pages and back. If you don't have anything on your own pages to link to, then you have one of three problems to rectify:

- You don't have enough content
- Your content is too unfocused, or
- Your content isn't useful enough to be linked to

The second type includes links that go from your pages to someone else's. Offering this type is very useful to your visitor, and crawlers look kindly on people who provide services to visitors. Be selective. Crawlers have started penalizing for pages and pages of random links. Make sure the content you intend to link to is relevant to your topic. Check regularly to make sure the links haven't broken. These can appear on dedicated resource pages, or as small text links in your articles (embedded links) or even FAQs that offer more information right where the person is reading.

The third type is the hardest. These are links from other people's sites to yours. The more relevant the content of the site linking to yours the better your site will rank. The engines also use the rank of the site linking to you to help determine the value of the link. Quality over quantity. How do you get links? Find sites you feel are worth linking to and contact the owners. You can use the search engines to do this, but you can also meet people at club meetings, conferences and other things. Start looking for partners. In this day and age, your competitors are also your partners. This is especially true for authors. After all, how many genre fiction readers do you know who read one author exclusively? How many researchers rely only on one source book? There's always room for more. Help each other.

> **Trick**
>
> When someone links to your site, go to the search engine url request pages and submit the site that linked to yours. The crawler will find your site through theirs and up your ranking.

You can check on who is linking to you. Go to Google and type in:

> link: your url

5.1.5 Other Meta Tag Keywording Efforts

We've already talked about the title tag. There are two other meta tags of import to mention. The description tag should be one or two brief, complete sentences telling what the page is about. If it's your home page, should give an overview of the content for the whole site. Sub pages get tailored sentences for their content. The keywords tag gets a list of key words and phrases related to that page. The crawlers look for matches between the tags and the content. Be mindful. They stop reading after 256 characters, so anything after that is wasted. Focus on what's important.

```
<HEAD>
<TITLE>Title of your site</TITLE>
<meta name="description" content="What your site is about.">
<meta name="keywords" content="relevant words, or, phrases">
</HEAD>
```

There are two more things you can do with keywords and these are best done when actually building the pages (or posting the blog posts), though websites can be retrofitted to do this.

Make your file names work for you. With the exception of your index file, which must always be named "index," all other files on your site can have unique names. Can you guess what these file names should contain? Instead of a file name like "links.html," try "cat_health_links.html."

As simplistic as that sounds, do you have any idea how many sites *do not* do this? Luckily for blog posts, they do use keywords in their titles or in the subdirectories where those articles are contained. Do you know where those words are pulled from? The headlines, or the titles you select for your articles. That is why your article titles are so important. WordPress now allows you to change the page title so you can streamline it to your needs. Any PDFs you put up should also have useful names, as should your mp3 files or anything else you're offering.

Which brings us to the other keywording opportunity you shouldn't waste: images. More specifically, image file names and alt tags. Have you ever used Google's image search feature? Wonder how it knows what those images are pictures of? Well, it isn't because it can view them. In fact, any text you put into an image on your site is hidden from crawlers, which is why you want to avoid flash or image files as headers, navigation and text content whenever possible. What the crawlers *can* see are the image names and the alt tags associated with them. So instead of naming your image "image1.gif," try "cat_health_healthy_heart.gif."

The alt tag is the text that you see when you hover over an image. It is also visible to crawlers and to people reliant on readers if your image is clickable. So instead of leaving it blank, put something useful in it.

5.1.6 RSS

RSS *(really simple syndication)* will automatically send your post to whoever subscribes to the feed. This is true for text posts as well as audio or video. Easy access to RSS distribution feeds is one of the reasons going with a hosted blogging platform is so attractive. Most blog software offers the ability to deliver an RSS feed. You can offer RSS through a website or through a service as well, but the blog platforms have made it RRSS *(really, really simple syndication)*. All you have to do is check a few boxes when setting up your account and your articles are syndicated throughout the web. I recommend that you enable the feature that only syndicates a paragraph or two and then provides a link to the full article on your blog. That way you can keep better track of the numbers and potentially attach the readers as regulars.

5.1.7 Longevity

Our last SEO secret is longevity. Longevity on the web counts, and not just because you've had more time to put in the content and get links to your stuff. There are date tags embedded in your files. The crawlers know how fresh your pages are. They also know how long your domain name has been around and the date it expires. If you're new to the web, buy your domain name for two to five years. It'll help. If you feel the urge, there are places where you can buy existing domain names at auction. These will bring longevity and residual traffic with them. I put a url in the resources list where you can shop for these. There are other places as well.

Having more than one domain name pointing to your same site is fine. But it's be even better to have a slight variation of your content on each domain name and have them all link together.

You want to know another dirty little secret? There is a magic number on the web and that number is 18—months to be exact. If you put up a website and do absolutely nothing to it, in 18 months your traffic is going to pick up. No joke. You may not get top placement in the search rankings, but you will start coming up in the results. If your topic is particularly competitive, this isn't going to mean much, but it helps. That's why it's important to secure your domain name and put *something* up as soon as possible. You need to hit that magic 18 as quickly as you can. Use those 18 months to practice the advice I've just given you and you'll be in good shape.

To help you focus on keywords and relevancy, fill out Worksheet 5.1.

Worksheet 5.1

Site Focus and Keywords

What does/do my site/s need to do for me? _____
_____
_____
_____

What topics could I focus my content on to accomplish this? _____
_____
_____
_____

Which of these topics do I have the most to say about? _____
_____
_____
_____

Should I have more than one site? _____ What would each site be focused on?
_____

If you were looking for the information you plan to present, what words or phrases would you type into a search engine box? _____
_____
_____
_____

If you knew nothing about your topic and needed information on it, what would you type into the keyword box? _____
_____
_____
_____

If you don't yet have a web presence, or you only have a website or a blog and not both, pay particular attention to the keywords. The very first place a search engine takes keyword relevancy is from the domain name. www.cathealthtips.com is going to automatically score higher than www.jolineskittycorner.com when someone searches for cat health.

So let's discuss keywords. "Keyword" is a misnomer. If you've ever typed a single word into a search engine, you'll quickly discover why. There's too much information out there. Do a search for "cat," and the results will be everything from kitten images to the Caterpillar construction equipment company. LiveSearch, which I happen to like better than Google, helpfully offers up some related searches. Try it and you'll notice that these are not single words. You'll get better results by typing in a key*phrase*.

All search engine optimization amounts to, is anticipating what someone interested in your material might type into a search engine box, and then making sure those words are included in your site. The most difficult part is figuring out what people are searching for. The good news is that the search engines know this information, hence the "related searches" offering. The bad news is that they aren't going to just give it to you for free—at least not more than the most basic information. That's where paid search comes in.

5.2 Paid Search

Take a look at my cat search on the next page. See those "Sponsored Links?" People paid for these. Not only do these links appear on search engine results, they also appear on blogs and other places that have subscribed to display them for a kick-back. Anyone here with a blog seen the option to get paid to display targeted advertising on their site? This is where it originates, at least some of it.

While I don't advocate relying on paid search, it has its uses, especially for a brand new site. Here's how it works.

Google AdWords, while not the only service available, is the most well known. I've included links to the MSN and Yahoo versions of this in the resources list. Basically, what you do is select a few keywords and phrases. AdWords then gives you some basic data on those phrases and offers related ones. You select a few. Try three to five for starters. You'll then bid a certain amount of money per click—$.10 minimum. AdWords (or whichever platform you're using) will estimate your ad placement based

Angela Render

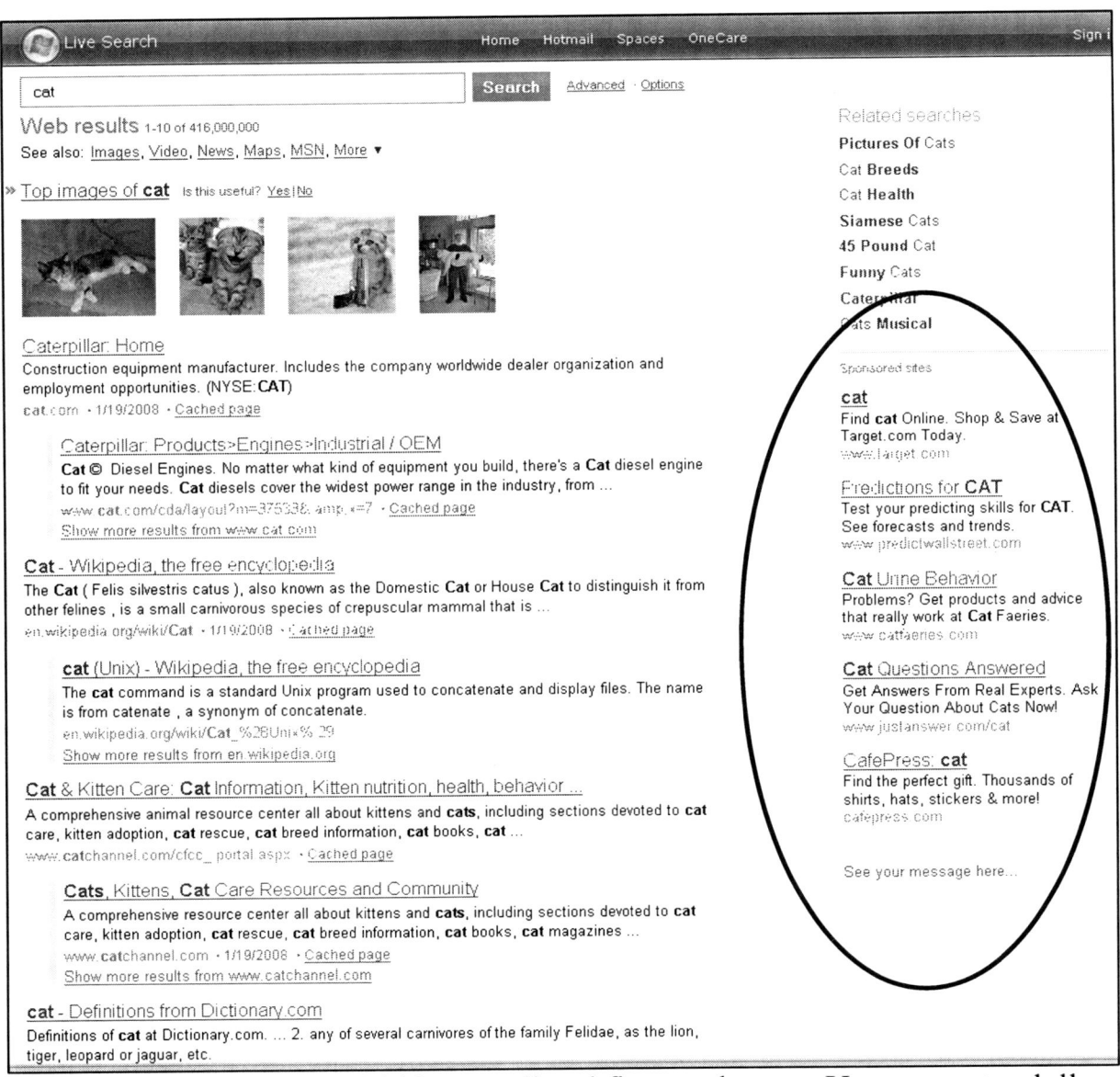

[Screenshot of a Live Search results page for "cat" with the sponsored sites column on the right circled.]

on your bid. The highest bidder gets listed first, and so on. You can put a dollar cap on your spending per month, or on the number of times your ad is displayed a day.

You can use this to get started on your keywording by clicking on the link to "Get Keyword Ideas." Google changes its offerings frequently, as well as the pages on which they're located. (Register this workbook at registration.angelarender.com and receive free updates.)

You can type in a few keywords you've thought of, or you can use the second option, which allows you to type in the url of competitors and click to get an idea of what keywords they're using. It will also offer some rudimentary traffic statistics—average search volume and trends by month over a year. It's not very much, but it's better than nothing.

This will get you started. But to really capitalize on this, you need to run some tests and get actual data based on your own webpages. Don't lose sight of the ultimate goal, though. You need to use this data to refine your organic SEO so that you don't have to rely on paid advertisements.

You do that by running a one to three month ad campaign. At the end of the period, look at your click-through statistics and see how the keyword is actually performing. If you can design unique landing pages for each ad, you can verify how the ads are doing. If you offer a unique sign-up form on each or a purchasing option, you can then track conversions.

There are times when paid search is appropriate for non-research purposes. If your book or topic is relevant to a news event, or to a specific holiday or something timely and of short duration, a paid search campaign will get you immediate exposure.

We've spent a lot of time on SEO, but there are other ways of having your site found. Does anyone remember the second most important aspect of SEO? Links! Links from other sites will get you traffic without the use of a search engine or SEO. Any relevant site will do. Guess what? Your own sites count. That's why having both a blog and a website is a good idea. Your blog posts get syndicated and bring in traffic that can then click through to your website. You can link to your blog articles from your website and treat them as news articles.

You can join forums on your topic and post helpful comments. You might cite an article you posted on your blog and put a link to it. Minimally, you will have your website url in your signature along with a link. You do have an email address with your url, right? (yourname@yoururl.com) Every email becomes free advertising.

Join organizations on either writing or on your topic. Get them to put a link to your site on their members page. If they don't have one, get after them to make one as a member benefit. All of these links will directly benefit your SEO.

Other electronic ways to get people to your site:

- Join newsgroups on your topic. Most have rules about advertising yourself, but most won't mind it if you put your url in your signature. Minimally, you should have an email address that uses your url. That alone will help because clever people will assume that you also have a website with that address.

- Set your email program to automatically add a signature that includes your url in all email correspondence.
- Make a podcast or other recording of you reading your work, or of you speaking, and send it out on the web.

Inclusion of logos is intended to spark ideas, not imply the endorsement of the organizations represented.

5.3 Non-Internet Methods

There are numerous ways of advertising your book that don't involve the Internet: business cards, letterhead, meeting people, giving classes, lectures or seminars. You notice my url is plastered all over this book along with compelling reasons to visit my site? There are also book signings, conventions, published articles, and radio broadcasts. I'll go over clever ways of looking at these in Chapter 6.

Chapter 6

Advanced Marketing Concepts

6.1 Philosophy of Marketing

From a marketing perspective, the purpose of all of your efforts is to:

- Make a sale on the spot
- Collect contact data for later marketing efforts
- Drive prospects to your website

Once you get prospects to your website, you need to either convert them to customers, or collect their email addresses or contact information so that you can market to them later.

Getting that information isn't as easy as it used to be. Because of all the SPAM we get, every last one of us is cagey when it comes to giving out our email addresses. You establish a relationship with a prospect by following all of the advice I gave you in the preceding chapters. Offer something of value and they will ask to hear more.

Fill out Worksheet 6.1, Identifying and Prioritizing Data. While you do this, I want you to list things you know you can share with people. Then I want you to rank those things in level of value. I'll give you a tip. The lowest levels should identify the prospect's problem and offer information on what you can do to fix this problem. The highest level of information tells people how to solve the problem. I also want you to list people you know who can help you. Completing Worksheets 1.5, 1.6.1, and 1.6.2 will help with this subject.

There are fresh copies of all the worksheets available for download if you register this workbook at registration.angelarender.com.

I quoted Sun Tzu earlier on knowing your enemy and knowing yourself. I want to re-work that quote once again. "Know your customer and know yourself." We just went over a bit more about knowing yourself. If you don't know what your prospects want, ask them. Surveys, forums, blogs, social events, meetings and evaluation forms are all ways of getting into the minds of your current and future customers.

Worksheet 6.1

Identifying and Prioritizing Data

What do I know? _____

_____

_____

_____

_____

_____

_____

Who do I know? _____

_____

_____

_____

What is the priority of my information?
Level 1 (Offer for free) _____

_____

_____

Level 2 (Offer in exchange for information/contact permission) _____

_____

_____

Level 3 (What they will pay for) _____

_____

_____

_____

Here are a few ideas for things you might offer a prospect in exchange for an email address, or in exchange for filling out a quick survey:

- Whitepaper
- Calendar
- Tips
- Short story

One way or another, to capture and utilize your prospects' email addresses, you are going to eventually need an auto-responder. For some of the items, you can get away with sending things out manually, but for others, the tips in particular, you're going to need a service that will automatically send out your information for you at a specified interval.

> **Quick Vocabulary**
>
> Auto-responder: A mass email service that captures data submitted via a web form and automatically emails whatever message, or messages in series, it's programmed to send, at whatever interval of time is specified.

These services can cost $30/mo and let you step away from the minute aspects of managing your list. You are able to send news or advertising blasts to your list in any segmented way you like, in addition to letting it just crank away at sending out your level 2 offerings.

Don't abuse your list. Don't constantly hammer them with ads or they are going to unsubscribe. Value, value, value. You have something they want, remember? One nice way to handle your ads is to send out a newsletter or news blast with only teasers in the email and then a link to your website for the full article. Then you place your product prominently on your website.

Try to have patience. Studies have shown that a person has to see your ad three to eight times before they respond to it. You went to a lot of effort to contact these people. Take care of them and they'll stick around to see your ad enough times to respond to it. You want these people around for the long haul because after this book, you're going to have 10 more books to sell right?

There are lots of things of real value you can offer to your prospects. These items can also create a way for getting them to return to your site (and see your advertising) regularly as well as make them feel like valuable parts of the process.

Sample Evaluation Form

Rate this Class

Advanced Marketing – Given at the Writers' Center on February 9, 2008

1. Overall, how did you feel about this class?

2. What were your expectations for this class?

3. Did it meet your expectations?   YES   NO

4. What would you like to have known more about?

5. What would you like to have known less about?

6. Would you please take a minute to share your feelings about this class?

7. How useful were the worksheets?

8. Would you like to attend an all-day or weekend long seminar on this topic? YES   NO

9. WEEKEND   DAY

10. May I use this information to promote myself and my services?   YES   NO

11. Would you like to receive email notices of future classes or news items from this instructor? YES   NO

    Email Address: _____

12. Would you like to receive my 15 tips for writers? FICTION   NONFICTION

    Email Address: _____

Thank You!!!
Angela Render

Invite their opinions by letting them vote on a design update for your website. Prepare fun quizzes. Silly personality type games are nice to offer as well, so long as they're well done and are on topic. Try bulletins with brief fascinating facts, or pertinent news flashes. Get them talking to you and to each other through a forum. They'll bond both with each other and with you. Now they're friends. Friends help each other. You help them, they pass your information on to two friends and so on and so on and then you have a Faberge Organics shampoo commercial. Seriously, that's called viral marketing. Above all, since you're asking, really *listen* to what they have to tell you.

One note on personal privacy and mass emailing: the CAN-SPAM act of 2003 put in a bunch of regulations that you'll have to adhere to. Whatever emailing service you subscribe to will keep you in compliance. Most of the regulations aren't too bad, but one is of particular concern. You are required to include a valid postal mailing address. The auto-responders will append this to all of your mailings. For authors, that usually means a home address, and I know I'm not exactly comfortable with sending that out. The good news is that it just has to be a valid address, so a P.O. box or business address is fine.

Your biggest ROI (*return on investment*) is in making your web presence useful.

Here's another vocabulary term on capturing prospect data: squeeze page. A squeeze page is a webpage stuffed with marketing data, the sole purpose of which is to get a prospect to do something. That something is probably either buying from you or giving you permission to contact them by handing over an email address. Old style squeeze pages are ugly in the extreme. You remember the example I gave of a horrible page for people eyes in Chapter 5? Well, as much as I hate them, they do work. At least, they did work.

Web travelers are more savvy these days and the response rates to the traditional squeeze page are not as good as they used to be. A new style of squeeze page, called a hybrid or reverse squeeze page, has recently come into use. Hybrids are much friendlier and can even be mistaken for websites or blogs, but they have the same function. There's a link in the resource list to my blog article on the

> **Quick Vocabulary**
>
> Viral Marketing: Advertising that spreads from one person to another.
>
> ROI: (*return on investment*) The amount you get back in exchange for the level of time, effort or money you put into something.
>
> Squeeze Page: A web page stuffed with marketing data, the sole purpose of which is to get a prospect to do something.
>
> Hybrid or Reverse Squeeze Page: An article or series of articles with prominent prospect capture opportunities.

subject, which has some statistics on effectiveness. Companies selling squeeze page template products claim a 30-50% conversion rate. For those of you with no marketing background, that sort of conversion is astronomically high. I found that hard to swallow until I discovered some data.

Here's the trick to getting these things to work for you: timing.

The old style squeeze page performs best when prospects respond to an ad or an email or something that has already interested them in your product, hence the ridiculously high conversion rate. They were already in a buying frame of mind. The squeeze page closed the sale. The new style is better for a person surfing the web who came to the page through a search engine (either organic or paid) or through a random Web link. These prospects are in a research frame of mind. The hybrid squeeze page is designed to capture and hold their interest long enough for them to either enter a buying frame of mind or to keep coming back to you until they finally convert. Sounds simple right? The only way to know for sure is to test some of these out for yourself.

6.2 Free Advertising

Advertising. Without it, no one will know you exist. It's expensive, so you need to focus on what you can get for free, and honestly, the free stuff is going to perform better for you and lead to more juicy things than the paid stuff, so it's never a waste of time. There are three huge methods of getting free advertising:

- Media coverage
- Speaking (which you can even get paid for)
- Using your networks

Can I tell you a secret? This last aspect of marketing has been the hardest for me to come to grips with. Harder even than getting up in front of a group of people and speaking as an expert. I am by nature a loner. It kills me to ask people for help. Like the public speaking thing—which I chose to power through rather than ask for help from a group like Toastmasters—I'm learning to get over it.

The only way this works for me is to offer something in return. If I look at it as an exchange, rather than using my contacts, I find it much easier to swallow. Get in touch with your strengths and what you can do for people and you'll be able to ask for what you lack in exchange, or even for support through some of the more trying things you're going to have to endure.

6.2.1 Tele-seminars

I'm going to share one free advertising tip that is network dependent. I attended a year-long marketing course put out by RTIR's Bill and Steve Harrison, who are really big on tele-seminars. What does a tele-seminar have to do with selling a book? I thought the exact same thing. It's taken a while for me to wrap my own head around this, so keep an open mind.

Remember those email lists I keep talking about? You do know that there are people out there that already have some, right? Big ones with members who are interested in what you have to say. Make friends with these people.

Nonfiction writers, come up with a talk on your subject, maybe 30-60 minutes. Offer this talk for free to members of this friend's list. Now here's the important part. Have them register for the event in order to get the phone number and pass code to the call. A link to a Web form from the email message is all it takes. There. Now you have their data. Give your talk. Offer a package that you're selling. If you don't have a book or package to sell, simply use it as a good will thing so that when you do have something, you can invite them to another free talk and market to them. See how this works?

Fiction writers can utilize this approach too. I know it seems weird—what do you hold a seminar on when you're writing fiction? I had a rotten time applying this to me in terms of selling my novel. I'll probably end up doing one or two in a professional capacity, but I did finally have an epiphany in the shower. (What? Isn't that were everybody has epiphanies?) Offer a reading along with a Q&A with you. You might find a couple of friends and do a group reading. Pretty much any book event—even the autographing if you set it up right—can be done nationally over the phone. The autographing part would take setting up an online shopping cart with a special access url, and then filling the orders yourself.

You're not as excited about this as I am. Give it time. It took me several months to take it seriously. Oh, one other thing. These conference call services will record your call for you. You can post this recording on your site, syndicate it as a podcast, send it to a radio station as a clip, or even package it up and sell it. There are services available that will take that audio recording and transcribe it. Clean up the transcription and you have an article or whitepaper to offer.

6.2.2 Articles and Interviews

Any article you write and sell is free advertising. Don't look to make a living off the sales of the articles themselves: at $30 for a 500 word article (which is what some venues pay), that's less than minimum wage. It's the prospect data you can obtain from your byline that's important. That and using the articles to establish your expertise in your topic. Make certain that you have your url in the byline or bio. For those of you who didn't skip straight to this chapter, remember that I talked about having simple domain names? This is why.

How do you find the right markets for your articles? I recommend going to the library and walking through the periodical stacks from A-Z. Libraries are better for this research mission than bookstores because bookstores are arranged by topic, so you're going to automatically limit yourself. Libraries are arranged alphabetically. Keep an open mind. If you try to sell only within your industry's publications, you'll miss a large portion of potential prospects. If your target market isn't your peers, your prospects may not even read the industry publications.

Let's revisit my imaginary yoga expert's book. For article markets, you immediately think health, holistic, or yoga specific magazines. Well, how about this headline:

"5 Fun and Easy Yoga Moves to Do With Your Kids."

Which magazines will be interested in that? *Family Circle, Parents, Parenting, Women's Day, Family Fun.*

How about this headline? "5 Fast Yoga Moves to Jumpstart Your Day."

Working Woman, Working Mother, O.

This is the same article except for the intro paragraph and the headline. Same moves. But it reaches a different market.

How about: "5 Cool Animal Poses?"

Ranger Rick, Muse, Click, National Geographic Kids

Same article! The key to leveraging your time is to re-use as much of your work as you can. By the time you've adjusted the text to fit the new market, it might not even count as a reprint anymore so you can potentially sell the first rights four times. Cool, eh? Just make sure the article is significantly rewritten when you sell the first rights again. Otherwise, it's reprint rights, but that's better than a dead article.

Also, don't blink about giving up the electronic rights to these articles. You want your work exposed as much as possible. Until they let me know that I was getting a column instead of a series of feature articles, I had a bit of remorse over my computer business articles sold to *Writers' Journal* because they don't archive them on their website. What I wanted was to establish my expertise and I wanted as broad a range of exposure as possible. Now my six articles are tied up a full two months a piece—a year on the last one. On the positive side, since the articles are not archived on the Web, my chances of selling reprint rights are significantly higher. And the column thing is a great feather in my cap, as is the published credit.

When an online outlet publishes your article, put a link on your website to the article's page on their website. Let everyone on your list know it's there so they can check it out. Ask them to forward the link to their friends. Remember, it's not the article sale that's going to make you money. It's the book sales and the sales of your package that are going to do it.

Media coverage is not limited to print. I hope that didn't shock you. Radio and television will give you fantastic exposure as well. Start locally and find shows that will interview you. Healthylife.net is a great national venue and there are hundreds of talk shows that need guests.

> **Tips**
>
> Watch or listen to the show (or read the publication) at least 10 times before you query.
>
> Pitch to the producer or the program director.
>
> Watch the credits to find whom to call.
>
> Pitch more than one idea at once, but make sure they all fit on one page.
>
> Make sure you are the perfect person to be on the show.

There are two tricks to getting your articles published or landing an interview. The first is to remember that the media doesn't care about you or your book. Well, they don't. What the media cares about it selling advertising.

To sell advertising, they need readers/viewers/listeners. So, to get your spot, you need to research the target audience and come up with an angle on your topic that is of interest to them.

Example:

What do moms want? Fast, fun, healthy activities that they won't have to fight their kids over. How does a yoga expert get free advertising on *Good Morning America*? A ten minute fun yoga work-out to do with the kids.

See how this works?

The other trick is to remember that the media is into news. That means timing. Articles are either considered "evergreen," in that they are of interest at any time, or "timely," in that they are pegged to a specific date or event. An evergreen article will get bumped in favor of a timely one. Simple as that. Peg fresh headlines to holidays, seasons, or events. Register a crazy holiday and make up your own if you have to.

It's your job to convince the editors or program managers that your topic is timely, of value to their audience, and that you are the right expert to interview. Make sure you include what distinguishes you from all the other experts on your topic.

Take a look here. See all these fast, easy tips with numbers in the headline? "7 Simple Stress Soothers," "15 Ways to Stay in Love," "Re-do a

Room in 48 Hours on the Cheap," "5 Secrets of Happy Couples," "Look 5 years younger fast, no diet no surgery."

Quick easy tips will get you on the cover. They'll also get you interviews. Radio and TV interview segments tend to be in the under-five-minutes range. Pare your information down to its most fascinating, bare-bones minimum.

Notice how all these tips appeal to one of the five things I told you people want? Let me repeat them. People want to be:

- Happier
- Healthier
- Wealthier
- Sexier

Another common angle is secret knowledge. Tips that you can only get in this issue, or exclusive interviews draw people in because humans are naturally curious and don't want to be left out.

You notice another pattern here. Each headline keys in to human emotion. People also respond to fear. Ways to avoid danger or correct problems will also get you where you want to be, but beware. If your audience is kept at a constant level of apprehension for a long period of time, they will stop being concerned. Take our national security color coding system. We've been on orange or red alert for so long no one pays attention to it anymore, much less takes any precautionary steps. News stations have been feeding us the fear factor angle on any story they can find for years. In this day and age, humor will get you the most long-term mileage.

Getting interviewed by someone else for their article is just as good if not better. A radio or television interview is pitched in a similar manner to an article. Research the show and target your pitch. While radio interviewers are very good at giving you the opportunity to plug your book and your website address, television sometimes doesn't have the time. That's where you need to politely ask what will be presented on the "super." Super is short for "superimposed" and it refers to the colored bar that appears under guests or

Angela Render
Author *Marketing for Writers*
angelarender.com

interviewees and includes their name and possibly some other designation. Ask to have your book title and url included on your super.

Simplify. Streamline. Your pitch for these things must be clear, concise, pertinent, and timely. Worksheet 6.2.2 will help you outline some ideas.

6.2.3 Speaking

> **Tip**
>
> Write your own introduction. That way you are sure to get a good one. Don't rely on the host to know anything about you and don't assume that they'll be good at introducing people.

Probably the most lucrative method of marketing yourself is to give seminars and classes. Once you've established your credibility, offer to give some talks. Start out for free, then move up to paid. Worksheets 6.2.3a and 6.2.3b, Speaking Opportunities and Identifying Target Planks, will help you. The material you cover in your talks doesn't have to be new. It can be re-worked material from your articles or from your book.

Toastmasters is an organization that will help you get over any stage fright you might harbor and they'll also help you refine your technique. Apart from practice and figuring out a way to become comfortable with your own body, the key to giving a truly memorable presentation is through storytelling. This is where being a writer can give you a natural advantage. Stories immediately connect your audience with you and your message. They tap into the audience's imagery, senses, and emotions. Select powerful images or scenes and describe them: time, place, characters, problem, smell, sight, touch, sound, taste.

Act out parts of the story to keep the audience's eyes on you and not their watches. Vary the volume and pitch of your voice as well as change the cadence. There's a reason movies illustrate boring office meetings and presentations as charts, bulleted points and a droning, monotone speaker. Self-deprecating humor will temper your image and keep you from coming off like a know-it-all. Just be careful not to ramble. Keep the point of your story clearly in focus in your own mind and do not stray from it.

One of the best speakers I have ever seen in person is a Christian evangelist named Jason Frenn. I've put a link to a YouTube recoding of one of his stories in the resources list, but seeing him in person is even better. Jason has mastered the art of storytelling. He keeps the audience engaged and entertained and while I'm certainly not going to convert as a result of his message, I enjoyed myself and I remember him and his stories.

Jason recommends that you script your story and practice it to the point where you can adjust it on the fly to suit your audience. Your story should identify with your audience, give you credibility, make a lasting impression, and drive home your point. If it does these things, it will also sell your product or service.

If evangelicals aren't your speed, check out a copy of "The Blue Collar Comedy Tour" and study how those comedians speak. Most successful comedians don't rely on one-liners, though many have a signature joke. The best comedians tell stories and draw you in with details and human behaviors that we can all relate to. Jeff Foxworthy says that the best material comes from real life. Of that, the things that happen to you are going to be the stories that you tell the best and will therefore have the most impact. The one thing to be careful of when modeling a story after a comedian is that the point of a comic's story is to get a laugh. The point of your story needs to relate to the topic you were brought in to talk about. Don't let your stories take you off on tangents.

> "You might be a redneck if…"
> —Jeff Foxworthy
>
> "Get'er done!"
> —Larry the Cable Guy
>
> "Here's your sign."
> —Bill Engvall

Like targeting article, radio, and television markets, speeches and presentations need to be tailored to individual venues as well. Use worksheet 6.2.3c to focus your topic into a presentation. You'll want to outline several different angles on your topic to use in different venues.

Here are a few more tips:

1. While it's good to script your stories for practice, do not read your presentation from a script. Use an outline on note cards until you get it memorized.

2. A common mistake is to include too much information. In an hour's presentation, expect to cover no more than three points. Two-thirds of the presentation will be stories and case studies illustrating those points.

3. Remember to rehearse your closing and your sales pitch. This should be the most polished part of your presentation.

(Continued p. 104)

Worksheet 6.2.2
Headlines

Ways my topic can promote love, health, or acceptance: _____
_____
_____
_____

Ways my topic can make or save people money: _____
_____
_____
_____

Consequences of not knowing what I have to say: _____
_____
_____
_____

Possible time pegs: _____
_____
_____

Headlines: _____
_____
_____
_____
_____

Worksheet 6.2.3a
Speaking Opportunities

Organizations I belong to: _____

_____

_____

_____

Five friends and the organizations they belong to: _____

_____

_____

_____

_____

_____

_____

_____

Things these groups might want to hear about that I can speak on:
_____

_____

_____

_____

_____

_____

_____

Worksheet 6.2.3b
Identifying Target Planks

Continuing Education: _____

Classes or Speaking Engagements I Could Give: _____
_____

Clubs or Organizations I Could Belong to: _____
_____
_____

Article Markets: _____
_____
_____

Personal Web Presence Needs: _____
_____

Forums, E-Newslists, or Blogs I Could Participate In: _____
_____

Radio or TV Spots I Could Have: _____
_____

Any Other Activity that Could Put Me in Front of People: _____
_____
_____

Ways I Can Meet People Who Can Help Me: _____
_____
_____

Worksheet 6.2.3c
Presentation Outline

Title:_____

Opening Story (The story should illustrate your topic and allow you to connect with your audience.):_____

_____

Offer at least three solutions, tips, or myth-busts that you'll cover in the presentation:

#1:_____

Story:_____

_____

#2:_____

Story:_____

_____

#3:_____

Story:_____

_____

#4:_____

Story:_____

_____

Introduce yourself (mention the things that are pertinent to your credibility as a speaker on this topic.):_____

_____

_____

Worksheet 6.2.3c
Presentation Outline Cont.

Talk about the issues that must be solved and tell a story for each:

#1:_____

Story: _____

_____

#2:_____

Story: _____

_____

#3:_____

Story: _____

_____

Talk about the common mistakes people make when dealing with the problem and tell a story to show the consequences:

#1:_____

Story: _____

_____

#2:_____

Story:_____

_____

#3:_____

Story:_____

_____

Worksheet 6.2.3c

Presentation Outline Cont.

Talk about what needs to be done to solve the problem, taking care not to give too much information on how to do it. Use stories and studies here to inspire:

#1: _____

Story: _____

_____

#2: _____

Story: _____

_____

#3: _____

Story: _____

_____

_____

Closing (This is the sales pitch where you describe what you have to offer):

_____

_____

_____

_____

_____

_____

_____

_____

During your opening, discover if your audience came in with any preconceived notions or expectations. When I asked the people attending my class on Advanced Marketing for Writers (given at a writers' center) if they were writers, a full two-thirds of the class said they were not and had no intention of publishing a book. They were there for Internet marketing tips. Needless to say, I adjusted the angle of my talk on the fly to include things for them.

4. Involve the audience in your presentation by inviting questions or by asking questions of them. My favorite is to have them stand up and recite the Successful Author's Marketing Pledge with me.

6.3 Packages

If you've followed this workbook from the beginning, then you've probably noticed that a great many things that you can do to market your book will also make you money. To recap:

- Giving classes, lectures, seminars, or speeches
- Publishing articles in magazines

Once you get the hang of doing them, these are all paid gigs. Many give the opportunity to sell books, but you don't have to give very many lectures before you discover that there's a lot more money in talking than in writing.

Which of the following do you think is the easiest to do? Sell:

- 1,000,000 items for $1.00 each
- 500,000 items at $2.00 each
- 50,000 items at $20.00 each
- 2,000 items at $500 each
- 1,000 items at $1,000 each
- 1 item at $1,000,000

At a $.90 royalty, you'll have to sell over one million books to be a millionaire. Great speakers can make thousands of dollars for an appearance. If you sell your books at the back of the room, you'll reach your goal that much faster.

The marketing concepts I'm imparting all revolve around you and wrap you up in a nice, saleable package. Packages are where your money is going to come from. Nonfiction writers will have an easier time with this, but fiction writers take note. There's stuff in here for everyone. Remember, I consider myself a fiction writer and the workbook you're reading is part of one of my packages.

Can you imagine:

- Your book as a movie?
- Your own radio or talk show?
- Your own syndicated column?
- A TV mini-series about your story?
- An audio version of your book in Starbucks?
- A streamlined how-to book in Lowes?
- A streamlined book given out to employees in large companies?
- Your main character as an action figure?
- A t-shirt with your artwork, slogan, poem, or logo?
- Your tips in a journal?
- Your slogan on a hat?
- A tip a week calendar?
- Your slogan on a coffee mug?

Well, why not?

Think big. Be certain that your publisher is thinking about subsidiary rights (excerpt sales, foreign translations, audio books, movies, textbooks, and other ancillary deals) to your work. Most books aren't sold in bookstores anyway. Wal-mart and Costco are two of the biggest retailers of books.

Start thinking about how you can package your material so that it can be sold at a higher price point. Add things to a book as a value-added incentive to purchase today. A book is the lowest ROI of time, energy, and money that you can have. Don't think in terms of, "How much can I sell my package for?" Think in terms of, "What do I have to put into the package to get the price I want to sell it for?" I want you to stop thinking of your book as the pinnacle thing you're trying to sell. It's only a small piece of what you have to offer.

Remember: re-tool, re-package, re-use, and re-sell. Think about what you could be selling on a back table at one of your talks. Yes, your book, but if they buy today, can they have your daily tip calendar as a special gift?

Maybe as an incentive to buy your book after one of your free tele-seminars, you can throw in an audio recording of the seminar itself. The packages are going to take time to put together and the most cost-effective way to do it is to create materials as you try out each new marketing angle or platform plank.

Someone asked me at one of my classes if I had a workbook available. Guess what? I went to the bother of scripting my classes and collecting screenshots for fabulous PowerPoint presentations because that is exactly what I planned to do: create this workbook and the videos of my lectures so that I could package them and sell them later. The worksheets have already been tested and the content critiqued by my students.

The free tips you offer can be expanded to lectures, or put on downloadable calendars. Each calendar will also have your web address.

Packages allow you to use two other marketing tools: cross-sell and up-sell. Cross-selling is something Amazon.com has turned into a fine art. The "Customers who bought this item also bought," list you're always offered is a cross-sell. It's an attempt to get you to buy a related product or service. An example for you would be to offer to sell an audio recording of your lectures to someone when they purchase your book. An up-sell is an attempt to get someone to buy a more expensive product or service (example: offer the hardcover instead of the paperback or a package of CDs and book instead of just the book). Packages give you the opportunity to sell more to your loving and loyal customers.

I thought all this packaging sounded underhanded and corny myself until I slept on it a few months and then it started to make sense. Ask yourself this: do you believe in your work? If you do, then you are doing people a favor by offering them these things. Remember our pledge at the beginning of this book?

> **"I am a damn good writer. I have something valuable to offer. People deserve the *privilege* of reading what I write."**

The hardest part about any of this is committing to doing it. I've repeatedly mentioned that the most valuable asset you have is yourself. That's because it's so true! Your commitment to whatever ideas you have is what's going to make this happen. Use worksheet 6.3 to help you think about packaging your material.

Worksheet 6.3
Packages

What services could I potentially offer? _____
_____
_____
_____
_____
_____

What products could I create? _____
_____
_____
_____
_____

How could I package these items? _____
_____
_____
_____
_____
_____
_____
_____

6.4 Bulk Sales

In addition to packaging your material for higher price-point sales, consider creating a pared-down version of your product that you can sell in bulk quantities to corporations. Think about all of the promotional materials corporations hand out to their employees or potential customers. Somebody has to write that stuff and the ideas do not have to originate internally to those companies.

> "Nothing could be finer than a really good one-liner."
>
> — Matthew Bennett

I had the pleasure of seeing Matthew Bennett speak on just this topic during Steve Harrison's Quantum Leap Program. He has sold millions of copies of his various products and has made so much money that he now donates half of his sales proceeds to charity. He did not sell those millions in stores. He sold them in bulk purchase orders to corporations.

The trick to doing this is to figure out how your information can be tailored to meet the needs of a corporation and create a product that they can brand as their own and hand out to promote themselves. In some cases, you don't even have to be an expert in your subject to do it. Matthew loves to tell the story of his first success, *The Maternal Journal*, which has over 3 million copies sold. *The Maternal Journal* is a pregnancy guide that consists of mostly write-in content (due-date, journal, etc.) with useful, basic information on basic topics. Matthew is not a woman, he wasn't married at the time, and he still doesn't have any kids. In short, he was completely unqualified to write this journal. But he did his research and presented a collection of useful information in a handy way. He then sold this to several companies. The biggest sales went to Abbott Laboratories (makers of Similac) and Babies R Us. These companies put their logo on it and handed copies out to promote their Brands. He likes to note that people accuse him of not actually selling all 3 million copies. Well, maybe he didn't do it one at a time, but he has the receipts to prove the sales.

The trick to doing this is to understand your target market. Matthew claims that if you have to convince the company that your topic is of interest to them, you are talking to the wrong company. For example, preaching to an environmental issues company that global warming is a threat is a waste of breath.

Like any other query method, you need to know what you have and what you want to do with it and be able to convey this information in a single sentence, at most in a single page.

Chapter 7

The Marketing Matrix:
Making the Aspects Work Together

7.1 Coming Up with a Plan

Now that your head is spinning and filled to bursting with ideas, you're probably feeling bit overwhelmed. No worries. This chapter will help you sort it all out and come up with a marketing plan that you can implement in nice, bite-sized chunks. For this reason, most of this chapter consists of worksheets.

There are three points I want to make before we do this:

1) Do not get so mired in this plan that you don't take advantage of an opportinuty when it presents itself.

The beauty of the marketing ideas I've given you is that one will open the door to another and you can never quite tell which opportunity it's going to be. Just be ready to move when it happens.

2) Schedule a weekly meeting with yourself (or, with a partner if you're lucky enough to have one). Assess the effectiveness of the previous week's efforts, adjust your plan to fit your current situation and then set new goals for that week.

3) Don't try and do everything in this workbook.

If you're doing everything in here, you probably aren't writing anymore and it was a passion for writing that drove you to this in the first place, wasn't it? Some of these ideas may not be right for you. Some of these ideas might not even possible at this point in your life. Select four or five based on what you already have and what you know—or who you know—and concentrate on those. Abandon what doesn't work and try new ideas as opportunities come along. Your time is valuable. If you aren't getting good results for the amount of time you're putting in, either hire someone else to do it or try something else.

To make the most of your marketing efforts, there are a few tools you need to have at your disposal, in roughly this order:

1) A free offering of some nature like a short story, report, audio recording, teleseminar, etc.
2) A way to get prospects to contact you and indicate interest. Probably a website.
3) A way to capture that prospect data: in person, on a survey, or on a website.
4) A way to sell your product: a brochure, website, or speech.
5) A way to follow up with prospects and build a relationship with them: newsletters, auto-responders, direct mail, an ezine, or a blog.
6) A way to fill orders: Amazon.com, digital delivery, Café Press, or ship stuff yourself.
7) A way to continue your relationship and sell to customers again: newsletters, auto-responders, direct mail, an ezine, or a blog.

If you are missing any of these items, making time to create them should take priority in your marketing plan, but should not take over your marketing plan.

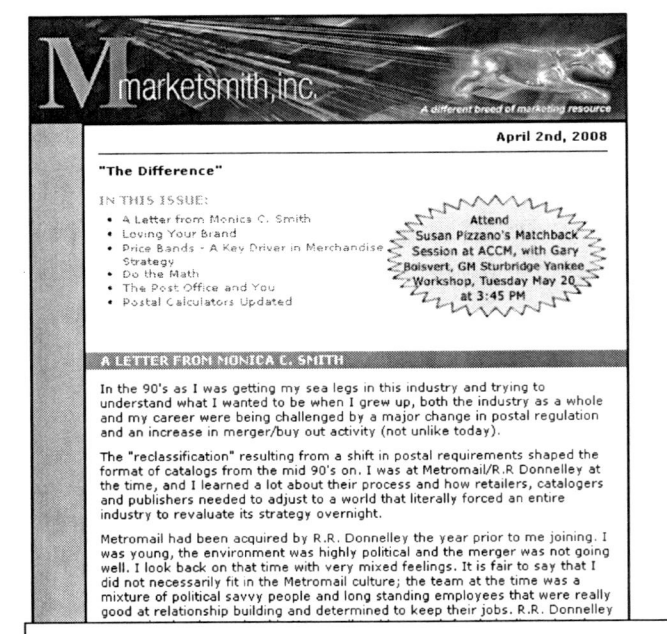

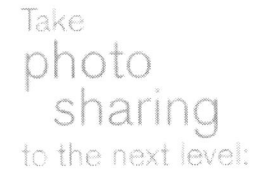

Here's an oversimplified flow-chart of how the marketing process works:

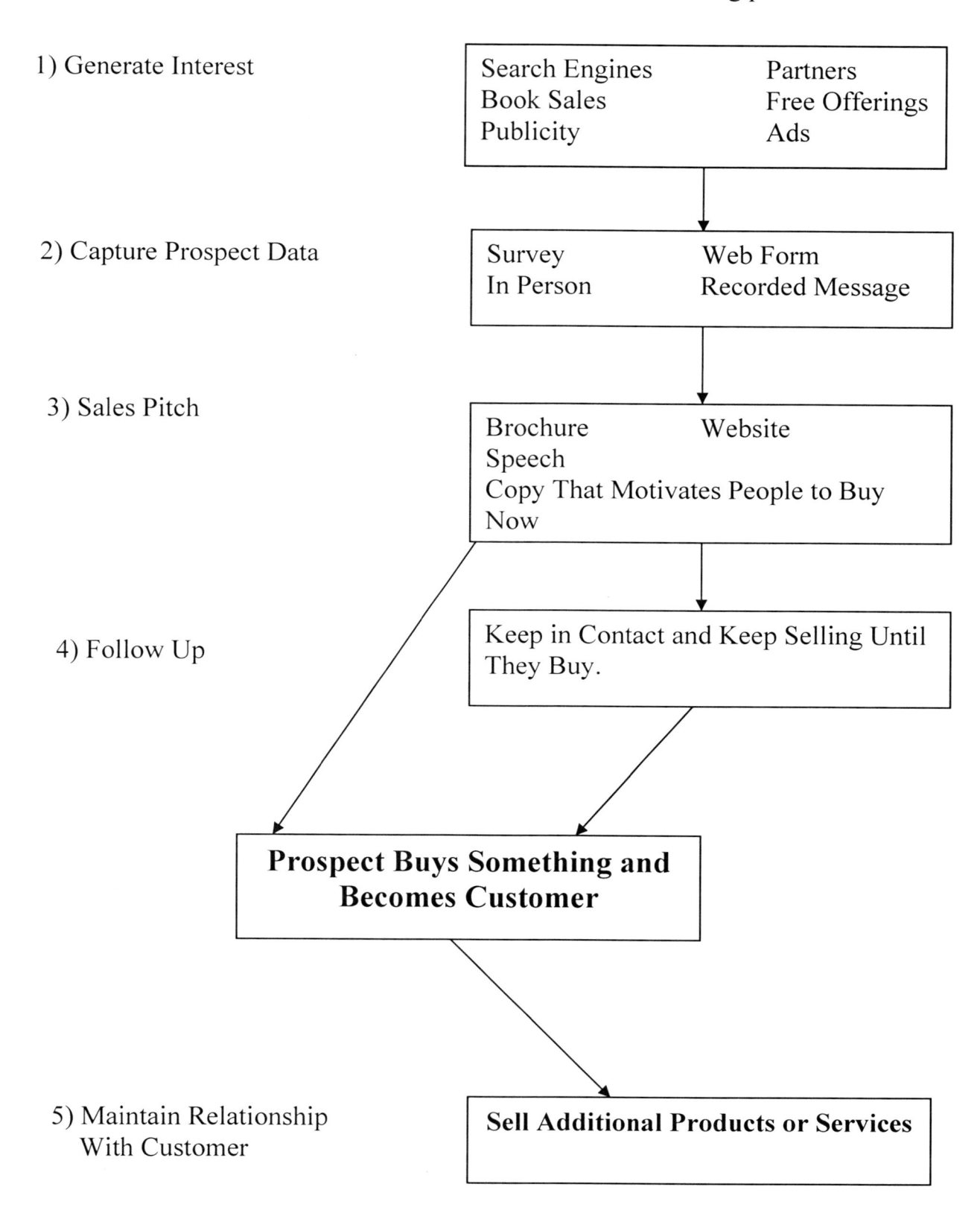

1) Generate Interest

Search Engines	Partners
Book Sales	Free Offerings
Publicity	Ads

2) Capture Prospect Data

| Survey | Web Form |
| In Person | Recorded Message |

3) Sales Pitch

Brochure   Website
Speech
Copy That Motivates People to Buy Now

4) Follow Up

Keep in Contact and Keep Selling Until They Buy.

Prospect Buys Something and Becomes Customer

5) Maintain Relationship With Customer

Sell Additional Products or Services

Take a look at the diagram below. Let's say you're giving a talk somewhere and the attendance is not guaranteed (like giving a motivational speech at a company). Maybe it's a class with no sales restrictions.

The chart below outlines a marketing plan in the microcosm. You can see how it all works. I want to start your first exercise in the *macro*cosm. Let's get a master plan going.

Sample Marketing Plan
Giving a Talk

Advertise Yourself
- Get the host to send to their membership
- Email all newsgroups or organizations you belong to
- Email your existing prospect list
- Ask partners to email their lists and offer an incentive
- Send press releases

Give the Talk
- Offer back-of-room sales of your book
- Offer free updates and news articles if they register their book with you
- Offer a free whitepaper of your speech if they fill out cards giving their email addresses

Follow Up
- Send whitepaper
- If they haven't bought the book, say that you can send an autographed copy if they respond by a certain day
- Follow up four times if they haven't bought, then put the contact on a long-term list

Prospect Converts to Customer

Ongoing Contact to Market Other Products Later

Now that you have a grasp of what needs to happen, take a stab at drawing a "big picture" version of your marketing plan. Use Worksheet 7.1a Master Marketing Plan to give yourself a rough outline.

Go back now and take a look at what you wrote down on Worksheet 1.5 My Existing Platform (p.15). Select up to four foundations and put them on Worksheet 7.1b Getting There. Then brainstorm ideas on how best to leverage those strengths to get to where you want to go. It's all right to repeat ideas for different foundations.

When you're done, get a couple of highlighters and mark the notes in the idea boxes that are the same, or that overlap. When deciding where to put your focus, select ideas that can be used for more than one effort. Use Worksheet 7.1c Promotional Ideas to help rank your ideas. Your answers to Worksheet 6.2.3b (p. 99) Identifying Target Planks will help with the follow-up column. You will need multiple copies of 7.1c and I urge you to *register this workbook at registration.angelarender.com* so that you can download PDF copies to print out.

Your tips will probably be high on the priority list. They won't take long. They can be used to start building your list, and they can give you spring-board ideas for articles and for blog posts, as well as for other products. They'll also force you to focus your topic if you're a nonfiction writer and can aid greatly when putting together a book proposal.

Collecting email addresses and contact data is one of the most important overall things you can do, so anything that progresses toward that goal will rank higher on your priority list.

Transfer each promotional idea to Worksheet 7.1d Steps to Goal and list each thing you need to do to make it happen.

Fill out Worksheet 7.1e Daily Promotional Goals at your weekly meeting with yourself and select one or two steps from your 7.1d sheets to focus on each day. There are a lot of coaches that try and spur you on by saying that you only need to spend 20 minutes a day working on this to see some progress. It's sort of like the businessperson's 20 minute workout. It sounds good on paper, but realistically, even a 20 minute workout takes longer than 20 minutes. You have to get to the gym, change clothes, stretch out, do the 20 minutes of exercise, shower, get dressed and drive home or back to work. That's an hour minimum.

The same thing holds true for your marketing exercises. Maybe you could get a call to two made on your break times at work, but in the mornings or in the evenings at home, by the time you've turned on your computer, sorted through what you're going to do, psyched yourself into doing it, focused on it and then shut everything down again, it's been an hour. That's not really a very effective use of time. I'm a writer. I know it takes about 20 minutes to get out of the external world and into what I'm trying to write. Is it worth 40 minutes of preparation for 20 of action? 30 minutes a day is better than nothing, but if you're strapped for time, dedicating a two-hour sitting once a week will be better in the time management department.

Then at your weekly meeting with yourself, fill out Worksheet 7.1f Weekly Evaluation and see how things are going. Use the results of that to come up with the next week's "to do" list.

7.2 Branding

Once you have a clear idea of what your product is, who your market is, and how it can be reached, you need to think about how you are going to brand yourself and I don't mean with an iron. If I said, "McDonald's," you'd all immediately picture red and yellow and a big, gold "M." That's branding. Branding can be a logo, a color scheme, a person (Oprah, Martha Stewart), a slogan (*Fly the Friendly Skies*), or a title series ("Chicken Soup" or "For Dummies").

The key to getting your brand to work for you is to use it consistently frequently. It doesn't hurt if it's catchy or visually appealing. Doing this takes planning. You need to coordinate your book covers, websites, business cards, and other print materials so that each reinforces the other. Don't feel funny about putting your brand on a t-shirt or coffee mug. Childrens book characters and artwork as well as comic book art are really good for this. Poets put a good, inspirational poem on a coffee mug and make someone's day brighter. Just don't forget to put your url on the other side.

Consistent action on your part will get you through the daunting laundry list of tasks that you have to complete. I am always looking for what works for people. If you discover anything that I haven't thought of while you're plowing through your own marketing plans, please share it with me. I would love to pass it on through my blog, my classes, new downloads, or even future revisions of this workbook. Contact me at: angela@angelarender.com.

Take care, and good luck!

Worksheet 7.1a
Master Marketing Plan

Ultimate Goal

Mid-Term Goals

Short Term Goals

Foundation

Worksheet 7.1b
Getting There

| Foundation 1 | Ideas to Leverage It |

| Foundation 2 | Ideas to Leverage It |

| Foundation 3 | Ideas to Leverage It |

| Foundation 4 | Ideas to Leverage It |

Worksheet 7.1c
Promotional Ideas

Idea	What is Needed to Follow-up

Worksheet 7.1d
Steps To Goal

Idea:

Goal:

Worsheet 7.1e
Daily Promotional Goals

What one idea can I focus on this week?

Day 1: _____

_____

_____

Day 2: _____

_____

_____

Day 3: _____

_____

_____

Day 4: _____

_____

_____

Day 5: _____

_____

Results: _____

_____

_____

Worksheet 7.1f
Weekly Evaluation

My Marketing Effort: _____
_____

What Happened? _____
_____

Why Success or Failure? _____
_____

Notes: _____
_____
_____
_____

My Marketing Effort: _____
_____

What Happened? _____
_____

Why Success or Failure? _____
_____

Notes: _____
_____
_____
_____

Resources

Articles

Do Squeeze Pages Really Work?
- www.angelarender.com/internetmarketingtips/2008/08/do-squeeze-pages-really-work/

How Often Should I Send to My Email Newslist?
- www.angelarender.com/internetmarketingtips/2008/08/how-often-should-i-send-to-my-email-list

How Many Copies is a Bestseller?
- tessgerritsen.com/blog/2007/07/18/how-many-copies-sold-is-a-bestseller

On Being Skipped
- antickmusings.blogspot.com/2008/10/on-being-skipped.html

SEO On A Shoestring
- www.imediaconnection.com/content/20646.asp

Audio/Visual Recording and Editing
- Audacity.sourceforge.net
- www.sonycreativesoftware.com (Soundforge)
- www.adobe.com/products/soundbooth (Adobe Soundbooth)
- www.mp3-wma-recorder.com (I-Sound Pro)
- www.adobe.com/special/products/audition/syntrillium.html (Adobe Audition Used to be Cool Edit Pro)
- www.fraps.com
- www.gotomeeting.com
- www.youtube.com
- www.audioacrobat.com
- www.idictate.com
- www.nuance.com/naturallyspeaking

Audio/Visual Syndication
- www.podcastally.com
- www.volcalo.org
- www.book-trailers.net
- www.youtube.com
- www.cosproductions.com
- www.watchthebook.com

Auto-responders and Email services
- www.1shoppingcart.com (If you like this one, I am an affiliate. Would you please sign up through my site? www.angelarender.com/clients)

- www.getresponse.com
- www.icontact.com
- www.citymax.com

Blogging Platforms
- www.wordpress.com
- www.blogger.com
- www.typepad.com
- www.livejournal.com

Books
- *Guerilla Marketing for Writers: 100 Weapons for Selling Your Work* by Levinson, Frishman and Larson
- *How to Use the Internet to Advertise, Promote, and Market Your Business or Website* by Bruce C. Brown
- *Photoshop Wow!* By Linnea Dayton and Cristen Gillespie

Crazy Holidays
- www.brownielocks.com
- Officially Register a Crazy Holiday
  Get a free application from:
  Editor, Chase's Calendar of Events
  McGraw-Hill Publishing Company
  Suite 900
  130 East Randolph Street
  Chicago, IL 60601

Domain Name Auction Site
- www.tdnam.com

Domain Name Registry and Hosting
- www.networksolutions.com
- www.godaddy.com

Finding Newsgroups
- www.ivillage.com
- groups.yahoo.com
- www.about.com
- www.ask.com (beware, answering these questions can be a time vortex and I'm not convinced of the value)

Google Resources
- adwords.google.com
- www.google.com/adwords/content-optimization
- www.google.com/adwords/optimizewebtools
- www.google.com/support/webmasters/bin/answer.py?answer=35769
- www.google.com/addurl
- adwords.google.com/select/KeywordToolExternal?defaultView=2

Internet Radio
- www.healthylife.net

Local Organizations
- www.writer.org
- www.marylandwriters.org
- www.washwriter.org

Nice Sites for Help
- www.problogger.com
- www.writerswell.org
- www.thegoldenpencil.com
- www.eriksherman.com/WriterBiz
- theurbanmuse.blogspot.com
- www.copywriterunderground.com
- catalystblogger.blogspot.com
- www.angelarender.com (Web Development and Marketing Services)
- www.ambitiousenterprises.com (Editorial and Publishing Consultation Services)
- www.toastmasters.org
- www.surveymonkey.com
- www.w3.org/WAI (Web Accessibility Initiative (WAI))
- www.authorsandspeakersnetwork.com/booksigningtips.html
- www.freelancersunion.org
- www.ezinearticles.com
- www.mediabistro.com
- www.spawn.org (Small Publishers, Authors, and Writers Network)
- tools.seobook.com/rank-checkers/seobook

Paid Search
- www.startadcenter.com (MSN)
- adwords.google.com (Google AdWords)
- searchmarketing.yahoo.com (Was Overature now Yahoo)

Photo Editing Software
- pho.to
- www.adobe.com/products/photoshop/index.html

Places to Create Mini Book Sites
- www.redroom.com
- www.shelfari.com

Places to Submit to Search Engines
- www.google.com/addurl
- siteexplorer.search.yahoo.com/submit
- www.dmoz.org/add.html
- search.msn.com/docs/submit.aspx

POD
- www.lightningsource.com
- www.lulu.com
- www.iuniverse.com
- www.booksurge.com

Printing
- www.overnightprints.com

Rights Free Images
- Microsoft Word's Onboard Clipart
- www.freefoto.com
- www.loc.gov (Some ARE copyrighted. If the photo was taken by a government employee it is most likely rights free.)
- www.archives.gov (Some ARE copyrighted. If the photo was taken by a government employee it is most likely rights free.)
- www.nasa.gov
- www.siris.si.edu (Some ARE copyrighted, especially if it's a photograph of a work of art. Ask them.)
- store.doverpublications.com (You'll probably need to purchase the book, but you'll get several hundred rights free images for $5.00. They have hundreds of books on different themes. They have free samples.)
- www.istockphoto.com ($5-$15/image)

Self-publishing Resources
- www.ingrambook.com
- www.lightningsource.com

- www.lulu.com
- www.pma-online.org
- www.greenleafbookgroup.com
- www.bowker.com
- www.isbn.org
- www.ala.org
- www.ala.org/ala/alsc/awardsscholarships/literaryawds/newberymedal/newberyterms/newberyterms.cfm (Newberry Award)
- www.pulitzer.org
- www.nationalbook.org
- www.bookspot.com
- www.nobelprize.org
- www.bookwire.com
- falcon.jmu.edu/~ramseyil/awards.htm
- www.bookexpoamerica.com
- www.midatlanticbookpublishers.com
- www.barnesandnoble.com
- www.amazon.com
- www.quality-books.com
- www.btol.com (Baker & Taylor)
- www.ipgbook.com
- www.openoffice.org

Site Traffic Rankings
- www.alexa.com

Social Networking or Bookmarking Sites and Services
- www.twitter.com
- www.facebook.com
- del.icio.us
- www.digg.com
- www.google.com/friendconnect
- www.nytimes.com/2008/09/07/magazine/07awareness-t.html
- www.comscore.com/press/release.asp?press=2396
- www.marketingsherpa.com
- www.marketingprofs.com
- www.ning.com
- en.wikipedia.org/wiki/List_of_social_networking_websites
- mashable.com/2007/10/23/social-networking-god
- hi5.com

- www.web-strategist.com/blog/2008/08/18/web-strategy-the-evolution-of-brands-on-twitter
- www.businessweek.com/technology/content/may2008/tc20080514_269697.htm
- pistachioconsulting.com/twitter-for-business-reading-list
- www.chrisbrogan.com/50-ideas-on-using-twitter-for-business
- www.chrisbrogan.com/make-your-linkedin-profile-work-for-you
- blog.guykawasaki.com/2007/01/ten_ways_to_use.html
- facebookadvice.com
- www.awcnj.org/media-tips.htm
- www.awcnj.org/social_netwroking_panel_10-24-08.htm

Speaking
- www.google.com/friendconnect
- www.toastmasters.com
- www.frenn.org
    - www.youtube.com/watch?v=BlTnhgEtCH8&

Tele-seminar/Webinar Services
- www.gotomeeting.com
- www.freeconference.comT
- www.freeconferencecall.com

Website Templates
- www.websitetemplates.com
- www.4templates.com
- www.citymax.com

Website Tracking and Statistics
- www.analog.cx
- www.google.com/analytics
- www.awstats.org
- www.webtrends.com

Who is linking to me?
- www.google.com search for **link:**www.yoururl.com

Glossary

- **Book Trailer** - Like a movie trailer. A one to three minute audio/video production advertising your book.
- **Breadcrumb** – A trail of links so that the person knows at a glance where they are on your website.
- **Callout** – Something you want attention brought to. These don't necessarily have to appear on the home page.
- **Content** - Anything included on your webpages that is not an advertisement. The more content your site has, the more relevant a search engine is likely to find your site.
- **Conversion** - Turning a prospect into a customer.
- **Cross-sell** – Suggesting a related product or service to a customer who is considering a purchase.
- **CSS** – (*cascading style sheet*) A method of creating a uniform look and feel on a website using a single file that is accessed from every page.
- **Customer** - A person who has purchased something from you.
- **DNS** – (*domain name service*) This is a directory listing that all of the other servers on the Web use to find your website. A system to match common names (www.yoursite.com) to the IP address(es) associated with that common name.
- **Domain Name** - Your website address. (ex. www.yoursite.com)
- **DPI** – (*dots per inch*) A printing term that determines how sharp a picture is. On the web, we use pixels instead of dots, but DPI is still used to refer to the resolution of an image. The higher the DPI, the sharper and larger the image is.
- **Embedded Links** – (also text links) Clickable words or phrases in the body of the text on a web page.
- **Footer** – The section along the bottom of the webpage. This will have a copyright notice, design credit and possibly a repeat of some of the more important navigation elements, or some less used elements like privacy statements.
- **Graphics** - Images. Anything on your site that isn't text, video or audio.
- **Graphics Editor** - A program like Photoshop that is used to create or alter images.
- **Header** – This tells the person who clicked on a link where they are. This needs to be persistent across your site.
- **Hits** – Hits include *all* files requested. Every image, every include, and every page counts as a hit, so one page view may be equal to 10-80 hits.

- **Home Page** – The first page people see when they type in your url.
- **Host** - The place where your website is located.
- **Hybrid or Reverse Squeeze Page** - An article or series of articles with prominent prospect capture opportunities.
- **IP Address** – (*Internet protocol address*) A series of numbers separated by periods. The IP address is the thing that the Web actually recognizes as your site. You have two of these. One is assigned by your registration company and it is that IP address that links you to the Web. The other is assigned by your hosting company (ex. 55.55.555.5).
- **ISP** – (*Internet service provider*) Your link to the Web. Whether you use a dial-up service like AOL or have a broadband link, someone has to know who you are and where to find you. Your ISP performs that service.
- **Keywords** - Words and phrases that can be used to refer to your website and its content. Keywords are used by search engines to help determine how relevant your site is to a person searching for something.
- **Navigation** – The links to get from one page of your site to the next. This can appear just under the header horizontally, or vertically along either the left or right sides of the page. This needs to be persistent or your visitors can become lost. The caveat here is for really big sites that have lots of easily categorized pages. These sites will sometimes have the main navigation across the top and then category specific navigation along the side.
- **Organic Search** - The list of search results presented by a search engine that are not paid advertising.
- **Page Views** – The total number of pages viewed on your site for a given period of time.
- **PDF** – (*portable document format*) A file format created by Adobe and readable by Adobe Acrobat. PDFs are easy to download, offer some protection from copying to the content on them, maintain their layout regardless of what program is used to open them, and are easily viewable by both Macs and PCs.
- **POD** – (*print on demand*) A technology that allows printers to cost-effectively print copies of a book only after the book is purchased.
- **Podcast** - An electronic audio recording that can be posted and syndicated on your website or blog. The term came from Apple's iPod, but it has come to mean any audio format. MP3 is the most commonly recognized format.
- **Prospect** - Someone who may be interested in purchasing your product.

- **PSD** – (*photoshop document*) An image saved in the format used by Adobe Photoshop.
- **Referrer** – The server that delivered your visitor to your site.
- **Registrar** - The place where you purchased your domain name.
- **Resolution** - The crispness of an image or how large an image can get before it looks blurry.
- **ROI** - (*return on investment*) The amount you get back in exchange for the level of time, effort, or money you put into something.
- **Root Server** - The central location to which all domain names and IP addresses refer. Network Solutions owns all the root servers.
- **RSS** - (*really simple syndication*) Automatically sends your post to whoever subscribes to the feed.
- **SEO** – (*search engine optimization*) is the art of making your Web presence easily readable and highly attractive to search engines like Google, Live Search, Ask, Yahoo, etc.
- **Sound Bite** - A short segment of an audio recording that is the "essence" of what that speech was about.
- **SMTP** – (s*imple mail transfer protocol*) This is the method the servers use to deliver email. An SMTP server is the place that knows your email address and can route your messages to you or hold them until you log in to pick them up.
- **Squeeze Page** - A webpage stuffed with marketing data, the sole purpose of which is to get a prospect to do something. A Web-based infomercial.
- **Sub Header** – Title of a secondary webpage or a secondary heading.
- **Sub Page** – Sometimes called category page. The pages reached from the top level of navigation. For some of you, this may be as far as any of it goes. These pages typically have a different organization to them than the Home Page.
- **Sub-Sub Page** – Any page organized below a sub page.
- **TIF, GIF, JPG** – (*aka. TIFF, GIFF, JPEG*) File extensions for images. Gif and jpg are more for the web and tif is used for print.
- **Unique Visit or Unique Page View** – Filters out multiple requests for the same page from the same requesting server.
- **Up-sell** – Attempting to get a customer to purchase a more expensive product or service.
- **URL** – (*uniform resource locator*) Your domain name or the IP address assigned to it. (ex. www.yoursite.com or 55.55.555.5)
- **Viral Marketing** - Advertising that spreads from one person to another.

- **Web Designer** - Web Artist. Designers are website graphics gurus. They can design a look and feel for your site. Some of them can program it for you, but some hand that task off to a developer.
- **Web Developer** - A person who can program a website. Some developers offer design services and editing services in addition to programming. Developers often work with designers.
- **Web Editor** - A professional who makes sure you've said what you mean and that you did it with proper grammar. Some designers and developers offer Web editing services.
- **Web Host** - Physical location of your website data.
- **Web Programmer -** Computer programmer. A person who can program or code a website, but who may or may not be able to design a site.

About the Author

Angela Render has been designing and maintaining websites for over a decade. She is a self-taught programmer who started out creating websites for herself, then moved on to programming for others. She was the Web Editorial Assistant for *Smithsonian* Magazine for two years before she was promoted to Web Developer. During that time, she received many commendations for her performance under pressure.

When her daughter was born in 2003, she gave up her position to become a full-time mom. Since then, Angela has taken on selected clients as her daughter's schedule permits. After four years, Angela decided it was time to expand her client list and is currently seeking new projects.

Angela also writes historical fiction, science fiction, fantasy and cross-genre romantica. Her historical novel, *Forged By Lightning: A Novel of Hannibal and Scipio* (ISBN: 1411680022 and 978-1411680029) was published in April, 2006. Her work has appeared in *Smithsonian* Magazine's website and she has a column in *Writers' Journal* called "Computer Business." She also teaches classes on Internet marketing for writers at the Bethesda Writers' Center and has appeared as a panelist and guest speaker at numerous Maryland venues. Her short story, "The Dryad," appears in the Maryland Writers' Association anthology, *New Lines From the Old Line State*.

For more information on Angela Render, visit her websites: www.angelarender.com and www.hannibalofcarthage.org.

Index

A

Accessibility, 65, 122-123
Advertising, 23, 25, 30, 47, 60, 66, 81, 83-84, 87, 89-94, 111-112, 126-127, 129
    free, 83, 90-92, 94, 127
    paid search, 72, 81, 83, 123
AdWords, Google, 81, 123
Affiliate, 39, 46, 121
ALT tags, 73-74, 76-78. *also* Meta tags
Amazon.com, 36, 39, 43, 46, 106, 110, 125
    affiliate, 46
Articles, 7, 11, 13, 19, 21, 30-31, 46-47, 52, 58, 67, 76-79, 83-84, 87, 89, 91-97, 100, 104, 113, 121, 123, 128
ARPANET, 40
Author's Marketing Pledge, 6, 106
Autograph, 11, 15, 23-24, 27, 37, 60-61, 91, 112, 123. *also* Book signing
Auto-responder, 87, 89, 110, 121
Award, 7, 39, 125

B

Barnes & Noble, 125
Bestseller, 12-13, 121
Bennett, Matthew, 57, 108
Bowker, 38, 125
Biography, 27-28, 30, 32, 44, 92. *also* bio
Blog, 2, 5, 11, 16-17, 19, 21, 49, 51-62, 69, 73, 75-76, 78-79, 81, 83, 85, 89, 100, 110, 113-114, 121-123, 128
Blogger, 53, 56, 121-123. also *Blogspot*
Blue Collar Comedy Tour, 97

BookExpo America, 39, 125
Book, 2-4, 9, 11-15, 17-18, 21, 23-29, 30-38, 39, 44-46, 49, 53, 58-61, 64, 66, 77, 79, 83-84, 87, 91-93, 95-96, 104-106, 110-111, 114, 121, 123-125, 127-128
    advertising, 23, 25, 30, 47, 60, 66, 81, 83-84, 87, 89-94, 111-112, 126-127, 129
    affiliate, 39, 46, 121
    audio, 28-29, 46, 49, 58-60, 79, 91, 105, 110, 121, 127-129
    awards, 7, 39, 125
    bestseller, 12-13, 121
    brochure, 26, 28, 47, 110-111
    business cards, 25-27, 84, 114
    cover, 2, 25-26, 28, 31, 37-38, 106, 114
    distribution, 12, 36, 38
    festivals (shows, expos, and fairs), 27, 39, 60, 84, 125
    marketing, 2-4, 11, 14-15, 23, 37-38, 44, 46, 104, 106
    marks, 24-25, 27
    platform, 2-3, 9, 11-16, 36-38, 106, 113
    podcasts, 11, 60, 84, 91, 121, 128
    print on demand, 2, 12, 36-38, 124-125, 128
    press release, 24, 28-29, 30-35, 52
    promotion, 11-12, 23-27, 30-32, 44, 53, 59, 84, 91, 93, 95, 108, 113, 117, 119
    proposal, 13, 37, 66, 113

publicity, 11, 23, 27-28, 30-32, 59, 83-84, 93, 95
publishing, 2-4, 11-13, 15, 23, 36-38, 104, 123-125
review, 2, 23, 26, 28, 38, 46, 53, 62
self-published, 2-4, 23, 36, 124-125, 128
signings, 11, 15, 23-24, 27, 37, 59, 60-61, 84, 123
stores, 2, 24-25, 27, 39, 46, 92, 105
test-market, 37
tour, 11, 23
trailer, 60-61, 121, 127
website, 44-47, 49
Books in Print, 38
Branding, 9, 64, 108, 114
Brochure, 26, 28, 47, 110-111
Business card, 25-27, 84, 114

C

Child, Julia, 52
Chat, 17, 59
Click, 93
Click-through, 29, 61, 72-73, 78, 81-83, 127. also *clickable*
Conference, 14, 77, 91, 126
    call, 91, 126
    writers, 14, 77
Conversion, 23, 111, 112
Copyright, 61, 67-68, 124, 127
Cover, 2, 25-26, 28, 31, 37-38, 114
    book, 25-26, 28-29, 31-32, 37, 114
    design, 37-38, 114
    letter, 28-29, 32
Crawler, 64, 68, 73-74, 76-79, see also *search, engines*
Creativity, 9, 60
Cross-sell, 106, 127

CSS, 65, 76, 127. also *cascading style sheet*
Customer, 9, 17-18, 23-25, 49, 85, 106, 108, 110-111, 127, 129

D

DARPANET, 40
Dayton, Linnea, 69, 122
Designer, 64, 76, 83, 69, 89, 127, 130
    graphics, 25, 64, 69, 89, 127, 130
    web, 64, 76, 83, 130
Dreamweaver, 62
Domain name, 42-45, 50, 55, 79, 81, 92, 122, 127, 129-130
    DNS, 127. also *domain name service*
    hosting, 42, 122, 128
    selecting, 42-43, 81, 92
    registry, 42, 44-45, 122, 129
    url, 56, 130

E

Editor, 2-4, 9, 29-31, 69, 94, 123, 127, 130
    graphics program, 69, 127
    copy, 2-4, 9, 29-31, 94, 123, 130
Engvall, Bill, 97
Email, 3-4, 11, 18, 24-29, 31, 40, 42, 46-47, 49-50, 52, 59, 67-68, 71, 83-85, 87-89, 90-91, 105-106, 112-113, 121, 129
    address, 25-27, 42, 47, 49, 83, 87 112
    Auto-responder, 87, 89, 110, 121
    bulk service, 28, 87, 89, 121
    CAN-SPAM Act, 89
    collection, 46, 85, 87, 89, 91, 113

    lists, 3, 24, 46, 87-88, 91, 121
    newsletter, 11, 46, 87, 110
    signature, 84
    spam, 29, 52, 59, 85, 89
    tips, 18, 46, 105-106, 113
Embedded links, 76-77, 127
Evaluation form, 85, 88, 114, 120
Excerpt, 46, 60, 105
Ezine, 110, 123

F

Family Circle, 92
Family Fun, 92
Feedback, 21
Fiction, 7, 13-15, 24, 37, 49, 53, 77, 88, 91, 104-105
Flash, 64-65, 68-69, 78
Forged By Lightning: A Novel of Hannibal and Scipio, 24, 37
Foxworthy, Jeff, 97
Frenn, Jason, 96, 126
FrontPage, 62
FTP, 40, 129 also *file transfer protocol*

G

Gillespie, Cristen, 69, 122
Genre, 7, 13, 37, 53, 77
Gif, 78, 129
Goals, 5-8, 22, 83, 104, 109, 113, 115, 118-119
GoDaddy, 42, 62, 65, 122
Good Morning America, 94
Google, 43, 47, 66, 68, 72-73, 77-78, 81-82, 123-126, 129
    AdWords, 81, 123
    Analytics, 66, 123
    search, 43, 72, 81-82, 124
Graphics, 25, 64, 69, 127, 130
    designer, 64, 130
    editing program, 69, 127

H

Harrison, Bill, 91
Harrison, Steve, 1, 91, 108
Harry Potter and the Deathly Hallows, 13
Healthylife.net, 93, 123
Hosting, 42, 53, 55, 66, 122, 128
HTML, 28-29, 49, 62, 78
Hybrid squeeze page, 89-90, 128

I

Indexing, 55, 64, 73, 78
Ingram, 36, 124
Interactive, 64
Internet, 40, 42
Interviews, 11, 23, 28, 31-32, 43, 58, 61, 92-96
IM, 40 also *instant messaging*
IRC, 40 also *Internet relay chat*
ISBN, 25, 27-28, 31, 36, 38, 125
ISP, 42, 62, 66, 73, 128. also *Internet service provider*
iUniverse, 124

J

Jpg, 26-27, 69, 129
Julie/Julia Project, 52

K

Keywords, 45, 58, 73-74, 76-83, 123, 128
Kirkus Reviews, 23

L

Larry the Cable Guy, 97
Lightning Source, 124
Links, 40, 46-47, 52, 58, 61-62, 64, 66-67, 72-73, 76-79, 81-83, 87, 89-91, 93, 96, 126-127
Lulu, 38, 124-125

M

Mailing lists, 11, 23-24, 29, 46, 59, 87, 91, 93, 100, 113, 121

Marketing, 2-6, 8-9, 11-14, 17, 23, 25-28, 30, 32, 36-38, 40-46, 49, 53, 58, 65, 72, 85, 88-93, 96-104, 106, 108-125, 130
- Internet, 40-58, 65, 72
- markets, 14, 23, 32, 37, 92-93, 96-97, 104
- packages, 104-106
- philosophy, 85, 89
- plan, 3, 5-6, 8-9, 11-13, 17, 25-26, 36-37, 49, 65, 72, 88-92, 96, 104, 109-120
- platform, 9, 11, 36-37
- pledge, 6, 104, 106
- research, 14, 17, 36-37, 41, 49, 65, 92, 108
- test, 37
- tools, 25-28, 30, 32, 40-46, 97-103, 106, 109
- viral, 89, 130

Marketsmith, Inc., 9

Mastering the Art of French Cooking, 52

Maternal Journal, The, 108

Media, 18, 23-24, 27-30, 32, 49, 59-61, 67, 71, 90-94
- kit, 27-29, 32
- method of delivering something, 18, 49, 59-61, 67, 71
- press, 23-24, 28-30, 90-94

Meta tag, 73-74, 76-78

Merchandising, 105

Microsoft, 61, 62, 72, 106, 124, 129
- FrontPage, 62
- live search, 72, 129
- PowerPoint, 20-21, 61, 106

Moser, Don, 31

Muse, 93

N

National Geographic Kids, 93

Networks, 11, 23, 25, 40, 52, 90-91, 123, 125-126
- computer, 40
- professional, 11, 25, 52, 90-91, 123
- sites, 125-126
- social, 11, 23, 25, 52, 90-91, 123, 125-126

Network Solutions, 42, 45, 53, 62, 65-66, 122, 129

Newsgroups, 13, 17, 83, 112, 122

Newsletters, 9, 11, 46, 87, 110

New York Times, 12, 23,

Nonfiction, 7, 13, 15, 49, 53, 88, 91, 104, 113

O

O Magazine, 92

Online, 13, 17, 26, 40-58, 65, 72, 83, 91, 93, 112, 122, 124-125
- booksellers, 46, 124-125
- marketing, 40-58, 65, 72
- newsgroups, 13, 17, 83, 112, 122
- printers, 26, 124-125
- publication, 93
- resources, 26, 93, 124-125
- sales, 91

Organic Search, 72-73, 83, 90, 128

Organizations, 16, 22, 29-30, 37, 39, 83, 96, 99-100, 112, 123
- genre, 16, 37, 83
- professional, 16, 22, 29-30, 83, 99-100
- publishers, 16, 39
- social, 16, 29-30, 83, 93, 99-100

writers, 16, 83, 123
Overature, 123

P

Page views, 66, 128
Parenting, 92
Parents, 92
Partners, 11, 58, 77, 109,
People Magazine, 31
Photoshop, 26, 69, 124, 127, 129
Photoshop WOW!, 69, 122
Photos, 29, 67-71, 124, 127
    copyright, 67-68
    editing, 69-70, 124, 127
    release form, 71
    rights-free, 124
Pho.to, 70
Pixels, 69, 127
Platform, 2-3, 9, 11-16, 36-38, 53, 55, 79, 81, 106, 113, 122
    author's, 2-3, 11-16, 36-38, 106, 113
    blogging, 53, 55, 79, 122
    marketing, 9, 11-16, 36-38, 106, 113
    software, 79, 81
POD (see *print on demand*)
Podcast, 11, 60, 84, 91, 121, 128
Postcards, 23-24, 60
Presentations, 20-29, 61, 96-103
    booking, 29-30
    handouts, 23-29
    PowerPoint, 20-21, 61, 106
    tips, 96-103
Press kit, 27-29, 32
Press release, 24, 28, 30-35, 52, 112, 125
    sample, 33-35
Print on demand, 2, 12, 36-39, 124, 128
Privacy, 46, 62, 66, 68, 89, 127
ProBlogger, 75, 123

Programmer, 28, 64-65, 68-69, 73-74, 76, 130
Promotion, 23-33, 44, 108, 113, 117, 119
    self, 23, 44, 113, 117, 119
    materials, 24-33, 108
    plan, 23, 44, 113, 117, 119
Promotional copies, 28
Prospect, 4, 23, 44, 46, 49, 85, 87, 89-90, 92, 110, 112, 127-129
Protocol, 40, 128-129
Publicity, 11, 23, 28, 31, 89-99, 111
    campaign, 89-99
    free, 11, 31, 89-99
    kit, 23
Publisher's Weekly, 23
    reviews in, 23
Publishing, 2-4, 11-16, 23, 25, 36-39, 93, 105, 122-124
    e-publications, 93
    print on demand, 2, 4, 12, 36-39, 124, 128
    registering as a publisher, 36-39
    self, 2, 4, 36-39, 124
    subsidiary rights, 105
    traditional, 2-3, 11-15, 23, 36, 38, 105

Q

Quantum Leap Program, 1, 108

R

Radio, 11, 13, 16, 23, 32, 43, 84, 91, 93, 95, 97, 100, 105, 123
    Internet, 93, 123
    interviews, 11, 23, 32, 43, 84, 93, 95, 97, 100, 105
Ranger Rick, 93
Readers, 12, 14-15, 27, 41, 51, 57-58, 64-65, 68, 76-79, 94

audience, 12, 14-15, 27, 41, 51, 57-58, 68, 77, 79, 94
software for the visually impaired, 64-65, 76, 78
Referrer, 66, 129
Registrar, 42, 53, 129
Reverse squeeze page, 89-90, 121, 128
Reviews, 2, 23, 26, 28, 38, 46, 53, 62
book, 2, 23, 28, 38, 46, 53
product, 62
testimonial, 26, 46
ROI, 89, 105, 128. *also* return on investment
Rowse, Darren, 75
RTIR, 91

S

Search, 5, 42-43, 45, 47, 55, 64, 67-68, 71-73, 77, 79, 81-83, 90, 111, 123-126, 128
engines, 5, 42-43, 45, 47, 55, 64, 67-68, 72, 77, 81-83, 90, 111, 124, 126-129
organic, 72, 90, 128
optimization, 42-43, 64, 71-73, 79, 82, 126-129
paid, 81-83, 90, 123
ranking, 68, 72-73, 79, 125
results, 5, 72, 79, 81, 128
Search Engine Optimization, 42-43, 64, 71-73, 79, 82, 126-129
Self-publishing, 2, 4, 12, 36-39, 124, 128. *also* print on demand
SEO (see *Search Engine Optimization*)
Server, 42, 47, 66, 127, 129
Shopping cart, 91, 121
Smith, Monica C., 9
Smithsonian Magazine, 15, 31

Social networking sites, 125
Sound Bite, 30-32, 129
SPAM, 29, 52, 59, 85, 89
CAN-SPAM Act, 89
Speaker's kit, 29
Speaking, 15, 29-30, 49, 96-104, 123
Squeeze page, 74, 89-90, 121, 128-129
hybrid, 89-90, 121, 128
reverse, 89-90, 121, 128
traditional, 74, 89-90, 121, 129
Sun Tzu, 9
Survey, 49, 85, 87, 110-111, 123

T

Tag, (see *meta tag*)
Target market, 5, 23, 26, 65, 92, 108
Teaching, 2, 11, 13, 19-21, 29, 69
Tele-seminar, 91, 105, 126
Testimonials, 26, 46
Test-market, 37, 83, 90, 106
Tips, 18, 23-24, 26, 46, 57, 85, 87-88, 91, 94-95, 97, 101, 104
base articles on, 94-95, 101
offer for email address, 18, 46, 87-88
marketing, 23-24, 26, 85, 91, 97, 104
web content, 57
Title tag, 73, 77
Toastmasters, 10, 20, 22, 29, 90, 96, 123, 126
Trade publications, 38, 92
Trade shows, 27, 39, 60, 84, 125
Traffic statistics, 65-66, 82-83, 126

U

USA Today, 23
url (see *domain name*)

V

Video, 28-29, 46, 49, 51, 58-61, 64, 71, 79, 106, 127,
Viral marketing, 89, 130
V-log, 11, 16, 51

W

Web, 3, 5, 15, 19, 25-27, 40-47, 50, 52-53, 55, 57-69, 72-74, 76-79, 81-83, 90, 92, 100, 106, 122-124, 126-130
- accessibility, 65, 122-123
- copyright, 61, 67-68, 124, 127
- crawler, 46-47, 64, 68, 72-74, 76-79, 81, 90. *also* spider
- designer, 64, 76, 83, 130
- developer, 15, 64-65, 123, 130
- domain, 25-27, 42-45, 50, 55, 79, 81, 92, 106, 122, 127, 129-130
- history, 40-41, 72-73
- hosting, 42, 122, 127-128, 130
- professional, 19, 41, 64-65, 123
- programmer, 28, 64-65, 68-69, 73-74, 76, 130
- traffic statistics, 65-67, 82-83, 126

Website, 5, 16, 23, 25-29, 31-32, 37, 39, 40-58, 60-67, 72-79, 81-83, 85-87, 89-91, 93, 95, 110-111, 114, 122-123, 126-129
- contents, 28-29, 31-32, 44, 46, 48, 60-63, 74, 83, 91, 93, 110, 127-129
- FAQs, 46, 77
- formatting, 61-64, 75-78, 127
- forms, 91, 111
- links, 47, 61-62, 64, 67, 73, 76-79, 81, 83, 93, 127-128
- marketing, 37, 40-58, 65, 72, 85-87
- SEO, 42-43, 64, 71-73, 77-79, 81-83, 128-129
- statistics, 65-67, 82-83, 126
- surveys, 49, 85, 87, 89, 110, 123
- url, 25-27, 77
- uses of, 28-29, 39, 47-49, 83, 85, 89, 93, 95, 110

Winfrey, Cary, 31
Women's Day, 92
WordPress, 53, 55-56, 78, 122
Working Mother, 92
Working Woman, 92
Writers' Journal, 93

Y

Yahoo, 72, 81, 122-124, 129

Printed in the United States
216463BV00001B/1/P